Real Venture Capital

Real Venture Capital
Building International Businesses

Richard Thompson

To Rheddy,

with happy memories and best wishes from

Richard Thompson

1. 4. 08

First edition 2006
Revised edition 2007
This edition 2008
Published by
PALGRAVE MACMILLAN
Houndmills, Basingstoke, Hampshire RG21 6XS and
175 Fifth Avenue, New York, N. Y. 10010
Companies and representatives throughout the world

PALGRAVE MACMILLAN is the global academic imprint of the Palgrave Macmillan division of St. Martin's Press, LLC and of Palgrave Macmillan Ltd. Macmillan® is a registered trademark in the United States, United Kingdom and other countries. Palgrave is a registered trademark in the European Union and other countries.

ISBN-13: 978–0–230–20222–1
ISBN-10: 0–230–20222–5

This book is printed on paper suitable for recycling and made from fully managed and sustained forest sources. Logging, pulping and manufacturing processes are expected to conform to the environmental regulations of the country of origin.

A catalogue record for this book is available from the British Library.

A catalog record for this book is available from the Library of Congress.

10 9 8 7 6 5 4 3 2 1
17 16 15 14 13 12 11 10 09 08

Printed and bound in China

'Esto perpetua'
Paolo Sarpi 1623

CONTENTS

ABOUT THE AUTHOR

RICHARD THOMPSON specialised in maths, higher maths and physics at Downside School and, after a National Service Commission in the Royal Engineers, graduated in engineering from Cambridge University. He then qualified professionally in both chartered engineering and management consultancy. He became a Director of the P-E Consulting Group in charge of its corporate strategy practice, before spending two years running New Court & Partners within the Rothschild Group. In 1977, he co-founded Thompson Clive & Partners with Colin Clive, and has been Executive Chairman of that international venture capital group since then.

In 1988, through a buy-out with GT Management, he established Pantheon Holdings with Rhoddy Swire, and was Chairman of that international fund of funds management group, specialising in private equity, for the first eight years of its existence. In 2005, he set up Solon Ventures with Angus Whiteley, and with support from Stewart Newton and Charles Richardson, and is Chairman of that company which has been formed to provide venture capital funds and assistance to UK healthcare and technology companies with international growth prospects.

Over the years, he has been chairman or director of a number of UK and US companies, some of which were floated on the London or NASDAQ Stock Exchanges. He has a wide experience of international business built up over a thirty-five year period.

He is married, has two married daughters and lives in London and Hampshire.

PREFACE

I FIRST went into venture capital over thirty years ago, before there was a venture capital industry in Britain, and in that time have tried to practise what I term 'real venture capital'. In my view, and hence this book's, real venture capital is trying to help companies achieve explosive growth in international growth markets by acting as a positive partner to the entrepreneurs and executives within those companies. To do this job properly, a venture capitalist requires experience in and knowledge of markets, products, technologies, management and finance which is, at best, a difficult combination to master, since it requires a long apprenticeship in science, industry and finance. Competence in finance is not enough.

In that thirty years, the venture capital industry in Britain, renamed private equity, has taken off and has been dominated by buy-out firms which now manage huge amounts of money. Whilst this sector has achieved good returns in the benign conditions for it in recent years of low interest rates and rising equity values, it is not real venture capital. It is instead concerned with the refinancing with debt of existing, usually mature, companies rather than the creation of new ones. Moreover, it takes the spotlight off real venture capital and siphons off much of the funding which should be available to that sector.

This book is, therefore, unashamedly a 'cri de coeur' for real venture capital, which practised properly, combines high reward with relatively low risk, since it gives the opportunity for an active involvement in companies. In essence, it should be the opposite of an old Lloyd's insurance membership with unlimited upside and limited downside!

My purpose in writing this book and stating the case for real venture capital also has several subsidiary aims. These are: first, to help entrepreneurs and executives to know what to look for and expect; second, to attract into the industry serious, well-trained people with more than a financial qualification; third, to encourage institutions to put their weight behind it; fourth, and last but not least, to help create a climate in which British inventiveness and technology can be properly exploited to everyone's advantage.

Whilst some of the content of the book has a British style and slant on venture capital, reflecting my origins and early experience, it is written for the international reader, as much as for the home one. Over a thirty-five year span of international operating and investing experience, much of which has been outside my own country, I have gravitated to become a convinced and committed internationalist, and I firmly believe that the principles and approaches put forward in this book are universally applicable, with sympathetic adaptation to local conditions.

The book makes liberal use of quotations to illustrate specific items and to illuminate the narrative. In some instances, the general sense of the quote, rather than its precise wording, has been adopted to make a specific point.

In writing the book, I have not included the names of investee companies with which I have worked as it would serve no purpose, since my aim in using examples is purely to illustrate the theories which I espouse and have sought to practise. My thanks are, however, due to the entrepreneurs, executives and colleagues with whom I have worked in these companies, many of whom have become friends. Without their involvement and help, I would not have been able to learn what I have over the years or to practise what I am now seeking to preach, in writing this book.

Thanks are also due to Cynthia, my wife, who has given me unstinting support over forty-four years in all the stresses and strains of establishing a venture capital company, and other companies, and of operating in a pressurised environment during my business career. The old chestnut of a venture capitalist coming home and telling his spouse that he has just been appointed the President of a client company and eliciting the response 'Oh, I am sorry, dear' has more than a kernel of truth in it, when things go wrong, which, of course, they sometimes do.

Next, thanks are due to Colin Clive who has been my business partner for over thirty years and who has played a vital role in developing Thompson Clive and a number of its successful investments. During this time, he has been a good friend and colleague.

Finally, I would like to thank all those who have helped in the preparation, transcription, editing and publishing of this book. Any errors or omissions are, however, my responsibility alone.

RICHARD THOMPSON

ONE

INTRODUCTION AND RATIONALE

I HAVE long wanted to write a book on venture capital but felt it was necessary to obtain sufficient experience before undertaking the task in order to be able to talk or, more accurately, write from strength. After over thirty years of practical experience, I believe that the time has come to put pen to paper before it is too late. In doing so, I realise that I am risking the wrath, albeit posthumously, of the Field Marshal who is supposed to have said 'there is a book in everyone but that is where it should stay.'

The book is intended to sit somewhere between a textbook and light narrative with an emphasis on principles and approaches. It is therefore more of a general, rather than a specific, treatise on the subject. Some of its material is based on a paper which I wrote for submission to the Wilson Committee on the City in 1977 and then presented, in updated form, to the National Association of Pension Funds at Brighton in 1984. This is included as Appendix I for the sake of completeness, although, since that time, my views have naturally developed.

The main purpose of the book is to emphasise the importance of real venture capital and to pass on what I have learnt. I do not pretend to have all the answers but, at least, I know what some of the problems are. Everyone has a system and mine, evolved over the years, has worked pretty well for me and has, I believe, the potential for a wider application.

A further purpose of the book is to rehabilitate the reputation of venture capital in the UK, which has become too identified with short-term exploitation and profit for the venture capitalist and its backers. Instead, it emphasises that the aim of venture capital should be to help facilitate the building of genuine growth

1

businesses which can have substantial longer-term benefits for everyone, including the national economy.

There is no short cut to learning to be a good venture capitalist and the starting point is an apprenticeship which covers an understanding of the scientific, management and financial issues involved in an investment and in the industry. When I was young, people spent more time painstakingly building a curriculum vitae over their formative years rather than looking for early success, which has become the prevailing culture.

Venture capital, properly practised, is a long-term business of partnership with entrepreneurs and executives and I do not know how this can be achieved without a solid understanding of business as well as of finance. The founders of good businesses are rare individuals with a difficult task, and they need help from a partner who can add real value to the project, often because the founder has not had experience before of some of the obstacles which need to be surmounted. People make mistakes when they are tackling difficult issues for the first time.

Contrary to current political behaviour and the drift towards a 'Nanny State', it is vital that we create new industries in the UK to replace the declining ones and this can only be done by rugged, self-reliant individuals who are determined to stand on their own feet and are frugal and conservative with money. It has been said that 'you can't run a big company if you haven't run a small one' and the reason for that is that you learn disciplines, particularly with finance, in a small company that stay with you all your life. State sponsorship and involvement in small companies is, invariably in my experience, a major disadvantage because it does not address the issues of survival and the vital importance of tackling problems quickly and getting things done. Developing a new company is like crossing a fast flowing stream in which you have to take one step at a time and one false move spells disaster.

Another theme that I have always been interested in is 'bridging the unbridgeable' which is how venture capital was created: as a bridge between industry and finance in the UK when these were much further apart thirty years ago. The key to achieving a successful bridge is for each side to understand the differences of the other and to work hard to make the partnership stick, rather like a successful marriage.

2

Other difficult bridges are cross-marketing over the Atlantic since many British companies fail to appreciate the sheer scale and competitiveness of the US market and many American companies do not reciprocally appreciate that their own model does not always work for more fragmented European and international markets, with their different cultures, languages and legal systems. Having said that, there are examples of brilliant successes on both sides, ranging from the Beatles to Coca-Cola.

A third bridge or, should I say, chasm, is that which has existed between commerce and academia. The climate has changed substantially in recent times, with the universities becoming much more interested, following a reduction of their government funding, in exploiting their technological assets. Many initiatives are now afoot and some of them show considerable promise. Indeed, the universities are now fully engaged in the commercial world, and the story of the Oxford don who is supposed to have said to a demobilised undergraduate, after the First World War, 'Was it you or your brother who was killed at the Somme?', would have little credence now.

Another big change that has occurred over the years is in the contribution required of a venture capitalist. In the early days of venture capital in the UK, he or she had to take a very active role in the investee company such as becoming its chairman. The reason for this was that there was far less interest in small private companies, both from executives and institutions, who were more attracted by the rewards of large public companies, and consequently talent and funds were in short supply for private equity.

Nowadays, the pendulum has swung completely and there are great attractions for executives and institutions in private companies, both because of the rewards that are available and the lesser burdens of corporate governance and public liability. The task of a venture capital firm in the UK is, therefore, more to pick good people to back, from the greater abundance of young would-be entrepreneurs now available, and to help them in a supportive, rather than a proactive, way. This makes the task of the firm an easier one and enables it to manage more money with the same resources, provided that it makes the right choices.

Turning to the content of the book which follows, it starts with a chapter covering the background and history of venture capital, before covering other forms of private equity. It then moves on to explore, in turn, venture capital definitions and approaches, growth markets and international expansion, the commercial application of technology products, entrepreneurs, managers and directors, the management of resources, financial philosophy and control and financing and its structures. Further chapters cover, sequentially, start-ups, second-stage financings, third-stage financings, turnrounds, strategic and other alliances, flotations, acquisitions and mergers, trade sales and case studies, illustrating the theories and statements. The next chapters of the book cover international niche businesses, international development, international financing, fund structures and management, investment processes, investment examples and future developments. The last chapters of the book deal with the role of the venture capitalist, the role of the investor, the impact on the economy and the conclusions and lessons reached.

Two

Background and History
of Venture Capital

VENTURE capital has a long pedigree and many people and nations are credited with its invention. Probably the earliest manifestation of it was during the Shong Dynasty in China over 800 years ago when the bidding organisation took shape. At that time, would-be inventors put their ideas to their village and the villagers bid for the right to finance them, keeping things in the family as it were.

Moving on several hundred years, the Merchant Adventurers and others were active from the fifteenth century in raising private capital for projects, often involving overseas voyages with the prospects of lucrative gain. The financing of these projects usually had substantial risks, exacerbated by the fact that the joint stock company, with limited liability, had not yet come into existence.

Modern venture capital began after the Second World War in the United States and its father is generally believed to have been General Georges Doriot who successfully commercialised some of the methods that he had used in the military during the war. It achieved its full flowering in the 1960s, with legendary figures such as Arthur Rock, Tommy Davis and others building successful firms that financed and helped technological advances in electronics, many of which were sourced from Stanford University in Palo Alto, California. This led to the formation of a venture capital industry in the US, centred upon 3000 Sand Hill Road at Menlo Park which was a complex of offices nearby put together by Tom Ford, the lawyer-cum-property entrepreneur, who recognised the industry's potential at an early stage.

In its formative years, the US venture capital industry was engaged in real venture capital, in that most of its early exponents provided scientific and commercial skills to new projects, in addition to the necessary finance, raised from individuals and institutions. As the industry grew in size and stature, it attracted very large funds, both domestically and internationally, and finance has increasingly become the dominant function for many firms, which is sad but inevitable perhaps. The dichotomy which exists between the original 'hands-on' concept of venture capital, pioneered by General Doriot, and the more passive financial approach, which followed in its wake, is an enduring feature of the industry, both in the US and elsewhere.

The US is an ideal environment for venture capital since it has a large domestic market, an emphasis on change and new technology, a surfeit of executives prepared to have a go and a large base of capital prepared to back new ventures. It is possible to build a strong domestic base for a new business, because of the size of the market, before striking out into the international field, with all its inherent difficulties and risks.

The US also has a large number of companies prepared to buy up early-stage ventures and a vibrant stock market in which new ventures can be floated. This combination of high upside and limited risk has produced some huge successes over the years and resulted in the US rightly being able to claim to be the home of modern venture capital. It still continues to dominate that world in terms of its successes and the amount of money that it manages.

Venture capital concepts and ideas crossed the Atlantic to Britain in the 1970s and a few firms, including my company, Thompson Clive, were formed in that decade. Previous to that, there had been much talk of a Funding Gap in the UK for small companies, starting with the Macmillan Report, which led to the formation in 1945 of the Industrial and Commercial Finance Corporation (ICFC), now the 3i Group, and the later Wilson Report on the City. Not much, however, was done to redress the problem, although spasmodic government initiatives were taken with tax incentive schemes, such as the Business Start-Up and Business Expansion Schemes and, more recently, with Enterprise Investment Schemes and Venture Capital Trusts.

In general, the results from these initiatives were disappointing, partly because they put time pressures and restrictions on investing but mainly because the creation of new companies in Britain is difficult, with there being a small domestic market. This requires companies to sell internationally at an early stage which, in turn, requires unique or very good products at a competitive price. In the US, a new company can achieve critical mass by good marketing, albeit with a moderate product in its domestic market, but in the UK this is not possible, and success requires early exploitation internationally of its products, which is a more demanding challenge.

Other factors, which have made real venture capital more difficult in the UK, are a resistance to change, a lack of emphasis in exploiting technology, a shortage of executives prepared to have a go in new companies, high tax rates and less experience of large capital gains. Ironically, Britain has a proud record of scientific and technological innovation but a poor one of commercialising its inventions, which are often taken in hand by overseas companies. A classic instance of this, in a different military context, was the Blitzkrieg theory involving the combined use of tanks and aircraft in overwhelming force against an enemy's weak point with a view to achieving penetration in depth, thereby creating chaos and the disruption of its command structure. This theory, although invented by two British Officers, Major-General J.F.C. Fuller and Captain B.H. Liddell Hart well before the Second World War, was initially not given priority by the British High Command. It was instead adopted and exploited brilliantly by the German one at the outset of the war.

Returning to the 1970s, nearly all of the financial effort in the UK was dedicated to the public markets, and early stage companies were viewed as risky, with little commercial value. The same thinking applied to careers where big companies, such as Shell, were seen as safe havens and a complete career in themselves, and small ones were considered very speculative.

In Continental Europe, progress was even slower due to a greater resistance to change, a more regulated society, onerous employment laws and a dominance of banks in the provision of capital. Stock Markets, at that time, were also far less developed for the raising of finance than in the US and the UK.

In the 1980s, some of the larger US venture capital firms invaded the UK and Continental Europe with what might be called 'the big company' model of venture capital in which the American style of ambitious strategy and heavy investment was applied to the European market, on the assumption that it was of similar size and make-up as the US one. These initiatives often ran into difficulties, due to the fragmented nature of the countries making up the European market and to their different cultures, ethics, languages and legal systems.

UK and other European venture capital firms faced different but equally daunting challenges in exploiting the US market since 'the small company' model had its limitations in the US, due to the latter's size and competitiveness. Where success has been achieved, it has usually been in a market niche which has provided some protection from the immense commercial pressures of the US business environment.

Recent statements and policies on enterprise by the Labour Government in the UK are long on intent but short on action, apart from some attractive tax incentives for investors. They also focus on the 'big company model' which is seen to be the one to copy and, whilst it has been successful in the US, it is singularly inappropriate to the UK national problems, highlighted earlier. These problems have been compounded by higher general taxes and increased regulation, introduced in recent years, which have made life much more difficult for small private companies. In fact, many of the admirable initiatives created by Margaret Thatcher, such as the rehabilitation of wealth creation, lower taxes and deregulation, which led to the effusion of an enterprise culture, have now been undone. This has substantial ramifications for the UK economy which needs a supply of well-founded new private companies which can become the international giants of tomorrow. A surfeit of public sector spending and job creation is no substitute for the real thing, or for real venture capital.

THREE

OTHER FORMS
OF PRIVATE EQUITY

I N THE early days of venture capital activity, both in the US and
in Europe, the emphasis on private equity was in backing new
ventures, usually with a technological flavour. As progress
was made and private companies became more acceptable as
investment vehicles, more and more funding attention was
focused on private equity as an asset class.

Because, particularly in the UK, new ventures were difficult to
make a success of, with several early venture capital firm failures
and disappointing results from government-led financing
scheme initiatives, other forms of private equity, in particular
leveraged buy-outs, came into favour in the UK in the early
1980s. The attractions of these, which involved taking an established business and leveraging it with bank debt, were that they
eliminated the start-up risk, often had management in place and
used large amounts of money on which, in good times, excellent
returns could be achieved.

Good times, in this connection, are when interest rates are low
and equity values are rising, which has largely been the situation
over the last decade or so. In this benign financial environment,
debt can be serviced and repaid with relative ease from cash
flow and the investee company's equity can be realised, after a
short period by venture capital standards, either through a
flotation or trade sale. The skills involved in this process are
essentially financial ones, which involve assessing a company's
cash flow and restructuring its balance sheet and, for this reason,
many exponents of the sector have professional accountancy or
corporate finance backgrounds.

The leveraged buy-out industry, although a perfectly good

business in its own right, is not venture capital in any sense of the word and does very little to create new growth businesses which are essential to the building of a vibrant economy. Leveraging can, indeed, increase the vulnerability of such businesses when economic downturns occur.

These buy-outs have achieved a dominant position in, for instance, the UK market because of the excellent returns many of them have produced in recent years. However, they tend to recycle existing businesses which often, after degearing has taken place, are refloated or sold on to another buy-out firm for a further bout of recycling.

I remember thirty years ago being told by somebody in the industry that he had 'the greatest deal since sliced bread' which seemed to me to be a very ordinary UK company with no growth or exports. Twenty-nine years later, namely last year, someone else used the same expression for the same company which presumably had been refinanced and sold on several times in the interval!

The buy-out role that the private equity industry is now playing has parallels with that undertaken in the past by companies such as Slater Walker which ran into difficulties in the early 1970s, when economic conditions reversed with rising interest rates and falling equity values. Other more durable proponents were the Hanson Trust which, with other conglomerates, prospered in the 1980s because of their tight financial management and eye for a deal.

With increasing competition in the UK and a surfeit of buy-out firms and capital, attention has spread to Continental Europe where there is a freeing-up of ownership attitudes and controls. Firms, particularly in the UK, are also taking direct control of companies in order to get the deal, in a sense playing the role that conglomerates did before they became unpopular in the City.

The dangers in the buy-out business are when there is pressure on cash flow and gearing becomes a vulnerability rather than an advantage as in, for instance, the retail sector in the UK in recent times. If these conditions spread wider in the economy as seems likely at some point, the buy-out industry could have its problems augmented by the weight of money which has been attracted to it in recent years. Like the internet boom of the late

1990s, too much money and too great an expectation have in them the seeds of their own regression. The conventional wisdom is, in the end, nearly always wrong and past returns are not always an indication of the future, as a longer-term study of history would show.

With, therefore, lower growth forecasts for the British economy and the possibility of stagflation, coupled with over-supply for the sector, buy-outs – although an established business – are likely to have a more difficult time in the years ahead. This could be exacerbated by some high profile failures involving large sums of money, particularly where a private equity firm has assumed a control position.

My main argument with forms of private equity other than venture capital is not in what they do, which is often valuable, but that they mop up a large amount of the capital for new ventures and channel it into the refinancing of existing, usually mature, businesses. They also take the focus off, and get confused with, real venture capital aimed at creating the growth industries of tomorrow. At the current time, it is difficult to name more than a handful of British companies which have achieved global importance in their sectors. Unless this process can be success-fully reversed, the outlook for the UK's economy and trade balance looks increasingly bleak.

This perspective is particularly galling when compared to the nineteenth century and the Victorian era which was one of scientific endeavour for the country and which made it the work-shop of the world. It was, I believe, Alexis de Tocqueville who said that 'the soul of a nation, that forgets its past, walks in dark-ness', or words to that effect. We, therefore, have to remember and be proud of our past and have to rekindle the spirit of scien-tific enterprise which we once had, but which is increasingly now being shown elsewhere in the attitudes and behaviour of emergent economies such as China and India.

Four

VENTURE CAPITAL DEFINITIONS AND APPROACHES

*T*HE *OXFORD* *ENGLISH* *DICTIONARY* defines venture as a 'risky undertaking' but, to me, venture capital is an investment with very high upside and varying degrees of risk, depending on the stage of investment in a company. In a world in which, for most people, money and time are scarce commodities, it is important to concentrate on situations in which the rewards are potentially very high and the risks are therefore commensurate with the rewards. The old adage 'nothing ventured, nothing gained' could perhaps be rewritten as 'nothing gained, nothing ventured' in this context.

Venture capital tends, in many people's minds, to be associated with early stage investments which is too narrow a definition, since it is often possible to get very high returns from later-stage investments with a lot of growth. A classic example of this is where a company, well established in its domestic market, is striking out at overseas markets and moving from a national to an international base.

The matrix set out opposite makes very clear the inter-relationships of reward and risk in venture capital for different stages of investment. The first three boxes represent real venture capital and assume substantial growth and upside, and the fourth box relates to mature companies which are the bread-and-butter of the buy-out industry.

Early-Stage	Second-Stage
High Reward High Risk	High Reward Medium Risk
Third-Stage High Reward Low Risk	Later-Stage Low/Medium Reward Low Risk

The early-stage box represents the well-known characteristics of start-up investments in which the company normally has a product but has yet to develop significant revenues and any profits. Since the risks are high, it is normally wise to limit the amount of money invested in this stage until progress is demonstrated. For me, high capitalisation start-ups are to be eschewed, as I prefer Bridge to Bingo.

The second-stage box would normally represent a company which has developed significant and, ideally, recurring revenues and moved into profitability. Its need for venture capital would normally be to power-up its marketing and management effort to exploit its potential mainly, but not exclusively, in its domestic market. Rewards must continue to be high and risks are moderate, and are mainly down to how the company is managed.

The third-stage box would classically involve an established company moving from a national to an international frontier, as discussed earlier. Provided international growth prospects are good, it represents for me the 'El Dorado' of investment, since it combines high reward with low risk, which is what most of us seek.

The fourth-stage box speaks for itself and is not real venture capital. It is filled by low or medium growth companies which are ideal vehicles for leveraged buy-outs, since they usually have good and reliable cash flows coupled with strong balance sheets. Bank debt can be raised, serviced and repaid, provided trading does not deteriorate, and the value of equity can therefore be upgraded before being realised, through a float or trade sale.

The three venture capital boxes all have high potential reward and varying degrees of risk. There is a theory that venture capital, contrary to popular conceptions, is the safest form of investment, since a venture capital firm has an active involvement with the companies it invests in, and can initiate some action when things go wrong in order to protect its investment. This contrasts with a public company investment in which all a disgruntled share-holder can do is sell an investment, if he or she can.

Turning from venture capital approaches to a specific invest-ment, the first thing to do is to satisfy oneself that the vision for the company, usually articulated by its founder, is exciting and credible and has enough upside. It was Victor Hugo who said that 'there is no limit to the power of an idea whose time has come', and ideas are the explosive force behind a successful new venture.

The vision needs to be expressed in a focused strategy which sets out the proper market and product policies for its achieve-ment. It is important that these should be clearly thought out and practical, since strategy without successful execution is a waste of time.

Behind a clearly thought out strategy for the vision, the people in business have to be right, both in terms of attitude and getting things done, and the projected financial returns must be attrac-tive, from a profit and cash flow standpoint. Cash flow is the life-blood of successful businesses and must be monitored very closely.

If all these facets stack up, a sensible price for the prospective investment needs to be negotiated on a basis which is fair and acceptable to both sides, probably resulting in the entrepreneur getting less than originally expected and the venture capitalist paying more than desired. In the discussions between the two, the added value that the latter can contribute to the cause, and the ultimate size of the cake which he or she can help to create, are vital to a satisfactory solution. A wise entrepreneur will look at the whole project, often covering a period of up to seven years, before choosing a financial partner, and should not just go for the highest value offer up-front.

Conversely, a venture capitalist will want to carry out thorough due diligence on a business before he or she makes an investment, as the relationship is likely to be a long one, and it is important to know what you are getting into. Such due diligence would normally comprise:

- a thorough review of the company's financial accounts and history, ideally of audited figures
- enquiries about the company's founder (where appropriate) and management, through contacting references and previous employers
- scrutiny of the company's products and technologies, with a clear understanding of their applications, preferably demonstrated in a live working environment
- analysis of a company's markets, through a combination of desk research and field interviewing with approved customers and industry experts.

The bulk of this work should be done by the venture capital team with judicious help, where necessary, from technology and other specialists. It should be supplemented by legal searches on the company conducted by the lawyers acting for the investors.

In making a new venture capital investment, it is important to have a clear idea of what the exit options are, if everything goes according to plan. These are very much subject to entrepreneurs' and managers' aspirations and intentions, which are sometimes hard to divine. Some people wish to build a big company ($1 billion is often the target in the US), and should be encouraged and helped to do so provided that they perform; others want to sell out at some stage and realise their gains which is a reality one has to accept and live with, where it exists.

Good venture capital firms should have a mix of commercial, technological and financial skills, as discussed earlier, and there is no substitute for business experience, if real value is being added by the venture capitalist. Instead of the adage 'if you can't do, teach', the relevant saying in a venture capital situation should perhaps be 'you can't teach, if you haven't done'.

In assessing a potential investment, the tangible assets such as the balance sheets, are much easier to deal with than the intangible ones. One of my theories is that the assessment of financials is 75% analysis, based on fact, and 25% instinct; that of people is 50% analysis and 50% instinct and that of markets and strategies is 25% analysis and 75% instinct. For these reasons, instinct or intuition, which is often deductive logic, is vital in assessing a company, particularly an early-stage one, and is often underestimated in importance. It is said that a great deal of thought is subconscious, often occurring during sleep, so there may be more of a logical basis to instinct than meets the eye, in that the options in a situation have been subconsciously evaluated.

The Athenians were, in their heyday, strong on deductive logic as mathematicians and it has always amazed me that Aristarchus, in the fourth century BC, deduced that the earth revolved around the sun, 1,900 years before Galileo enabled it to be proved. Venture capital assessment is much the same process, although hopefully one does not have to wait so long in order to prove the success of a judgement and an investment!

Staying with the Greeks, a good venture capital firm will have a mix of deductive skills to judge the concepts and intangibles, along the lines of Plato, and inductive skills to deal with the empirical and tangible ones, along the lines of Aristotle. It is the combination of these talents in a firm which is so important since, rarely, does one person have all the attributes required for a successful evaluation.

In assessing investment opportunities, and excluding the dross, about 10% of potential deals are excellent and ring all the bells, 10% are rotten and to be avoided and 80% are somewhere in the middle. The first category are clearly the ones to be sought and any in the middle ground should identify how weaknesses and dangers are going to be dealt with, since they will usually make themselves felt in the life span of an investment.

Other adages and guidelines are to back one's instincts, particularly when confronted by people who are certain that they are right, and not to back people who have the wrong attitude to money. If partners have a sensible and common attitude to money, all other problems can be resolved, but differences on money will blow most partnerships apart.

Finally, real venture capital is difficult and we all fall short on what we should do or should have done. However, there is no substitute for learning from one's experience and refusing to be discouraged by it. Determination and persistence are worth a lot, both in executives and venture capitalists, and usually win out in the end.

FIVE

GROWTH MARKETS AND INTERNATIONAL EXPANSION

I N ORDER to achieve the aim of unlimited upside for a venture
capital investment, it is vital to be operating in growth
markets on the basis that it is easier to row with the current
than against it. Since management and finance are limited in a
venture capital firm, it is important to apply them to growth
markets. It is also a waste of time to apply good management in
investee companies to low growth markets in venture capital,
although it makes more sense in the case of buy-outs and
development capital.

The US is the easiest market in which to build a new company,
since a base can first be established in the domestic market and
then, from strength, the company can strike out into the international one. In the UK and Continental Europe, it is more
difficult to build a growth business, since the domestic markets
are small and it is necessary to sell into other national
markets and go international earlier, in order to be successful in
this wider field. To achieve this, a company must have an excellent or very good product which essentially helps sell itself
whilst, in the US, a moderate product can do very well in its
domestic market with top-class marketing.

The classic growth markets for venture capital investment are
healthcare and technology, because both are large, have long-
term growth and are very international, with the US being the
largest national market in each case. In addition, the medical and
scientific advances that are being made in these markets at the
moment make them even more attractive than in the past.

Profiles, from an investment standpoint, of the healthcare and
technology markets are set out in Appendix II, with the former

being divided into pharmaceutical, biotechnology, medical devices and health information sectors and the latter into information technology, telecommunications, instrumentation and consumer electronic ones. The bulk of the Appendix was prepared for a lecture that I gave on International Venture Capital in 1999 at the Tuck School of Management at Dartmouth College, New Hampshire in the US. Whilst the figures and much of the material are out-of-date, the fundamental characteristics and investment potential of the markets, portrayed in the document, are broadly unchanged.

The healthcare market is the ideal venture capital market in which there is long-term growth, fuelled by rising needs and increasing longevity, and considerable product stability, once the product is established. An American President supposedly said that steering a piece of legislation through Congress is like getting a feather mattress up a spiral staircase: it is a terrible job to get it through but, having achieved that, one has the satisfaction of knowing that it will be an equally difficult job for anyone else to get it out again. A new healthcare product has much the same characteristics in that it needs to overcome major barriers but, once achieved, the protection is greater since any potential competitor has to go through the same process.

Healthcare products are, as intimated, very difficult to establish in the first instance, since regulatory approval takes time and the medical fraternity is slow to change and adopt new products, particularly where they affect human life. For these reasons, healthcare start-ups are risky and drawn out and tend to absorb a lot of capital.

Technology markets, on the other hand, are the reverse, with start-ups being much easier and quicker to achieve. They also require less capital and many successful computer or software companies, for instance, begin life as consultancies or service businesses which provide a self-financing revenue base on which products can be built and exploited.

Once a technology company is established, however, it usually has far less product stability and less protection from competition, which can launch itself equally easily. For these reasons, it is often necessary for a venture capital firm to exit earlier than it would ideally wish to do, albeit often after the investee company has achieved public company status. There are, of course, exceptions such as Microsoft which has created a unique technology and, for a long time, was in a dominant position in its sector.

A third very exciting dimension to the growth market spectrum is the convergence which is taking place between the healthcare and technology markets. In the main, the healthcare market has been slow to accept and apply technology but the situation is changing fast. This, coupled with the advances in biotechnology and the increased power of IT and other technology weapons, provides massive opportunities in the convergence of the two markets. For example, it used to take many years to screen a database manually in order to find a lead molecule for a drug, whereas now it can be done automatically by high-speed screening in days or even hours.

Other growth markets exist, such as the aviation, defence and leisure ones, and these should be judiciously exploited. From a venture capital standpoint though, the healthcare and technology markets provide the greatest opportunity, accentuated by the fact that they are converging, as discussed. Often the key for a successful company and venture capital investment is to have uniqueness in a combination of technologies, rather than in the technology itself, or in a combination of market and technology characteristics. Such combinations, like the mix of petrol and air in an internal combustion engine, can provide interaction and explosive growth.

It is not technology as an entity which is important but the commercial application of technology to solve a defined market problem or problems. This is the springboard to success, as discussed more fully in the next section, and can often relate to medium or even low technology products. There is no particular advantage in high technology itself if it does not meet a commercial need, particularly since its costs and risks are greater.

In order to achieve commercial success, a focused strategy must be developed for a company which identifies market opportunities to which its key products can be practically applied. In the case of small companies, these opportunities are usually market niches which can provide protection against big company competition.

Once success on a narrow front has been achieved, the company can consider moving from being a national to an international one. Such a development requires a clear understanding of different national markets, cultures, employment laws, regulations, taxes and financial sources and public markets.

Following the development of internationalising its products, the company can expand its product base organically and then, in due course, the process of market and product expansion can be accelerated by acquisition. It is normally wise for a company to concentrate on tactical acquisitions, which fit its strategy and can be absorbed in a low-risk manner.

Whilst organic growth is difficult and takes time, acquisitions are notoriously dangerous and only about one in nine of them is truly successful, since people tend to be mesmerised by the advantages which are normally few and large and overlook the problems which tend to be small and numerous. The best acquisitions are those that are relatively small in relation to the base business and fit clearly within the defined strategy, so that the industrial logic is clear and compelling.

It is wise to avoid a situation in acquisitions where the base business is threatened by a new, and less understood, activity and which, with failure, can sink the whole ship. In a different theatre, but a similar situation, it has been said that Admiral Jellicoe was the only man in Britain who could lose the First World War in an afternoon, since the loss of naval supremacy would be a disaster for the country. For this reason, Jutland was the only major battle fought between the British and German fleets, with a result that was generally considered to be inconclusive.

As a young company stretches its wings internationally, it is often wise to seek to become an international niche business with a worldwide market reach but a narrow and specialist product range of high quality, so that it can retain its flexibility and ability to move fast. This is a better model in today's changing world rather than to seek to be a big company, with major resources and overheads which was often the key to overseas trading in the post-war years, as exemplified by the dominance of companies such as General Motors and IBM in that era.

In developing such international niche businesses, company

managements and their backers have to understand the cultural and other differences which exist in different countries in the world. The aim should be 'to think big and act small' so that the entrepreneurial, creative and fast-moving nature of the business can be preserved for as long as possible. Like Henry V's army at Agincourt, the combination of a 'little body with a mighty heart' is the formula for success.

Six

The Commercial Application of Technology Products

I T IS NOT necessarily technology itself which is the key, and many people with no technology training go overboard on the subject, but the practical application of technology to market niche needs. Very often technology provides the basis for replacing an existing product with an improved method of doing things, which is the quickest way of establishing a new product since it is replacing an existing one, the need for which is already accepted.

Many such applications are medium and even low technology, rather than high technology, ones which normally require a very substantial level of research and development expenditure. However, they are no worse for that, since they are less risky.

Patents are clearly desirable and sometimes essential, as in the pharmaceutical industry, where they enable drug companies to recoup their substantial R&D spend on a new product over a protected period. For many small companies, however, patents are time-consuming to achieve and difficult and expensive to enforce. Often a more practical solution is to have an R&D lead-time, coupled with protection in the market itself, which, for instance in the healthcare field, is worth a lot.

Very rarely is a particular technology unique in a commercial setting. More often a situation exists where there is a combination of established technologies which mix together in a practical and successful way to achieve results. In such situations, it is therefore the combination of technologies which is unique.

An ideal application of this is the healthcare field, where advances in biotechnology are harnessed to the power of IT processing. This combination enables things to be done which, in the past, could only be dreamed about.

New products in the healthcare field are difficult to develop because of regulatory requirements of statutory bodies, such as the US Federal Drug Administration, and also the natural reluctance of the medical infrastructure to accept changes which affect human life. They therefore take a lot of time to develop, usually far longer than anticipated, and require heavy funding.

Once new healthcare products have been successfully established, they do have, however, substantial product stability since the obstacles which have been overcome to get there act as a brake on aspiring competitors. The medical fraternity also tends to favour established solutions which do not have adverse risks to human life.

IT products conversely are relatively easy and inexpensive to develop to the benefit of technology start-ups. These classically range from a company starting in a garage in order to build hardware in the old days of the computer industry to one now starting on consultancy or on services, and then developing products on the back of that revenue stream.

IT products do, however, have relatively little product stability compared, for instance, to healthcare ones and, once developed, are open to competitive challenge, unless a unique technology format is evolved as Microsoft managed to achieve. Successful investment in the market, therefore, tends to produce quicker lift-offs for new companies but earlier exits, particularly once a company has gone public.

Initiatives in new products can either be market-led, or product-led with a unique technology or, more likely, a combination of technologies. In the first case, market relationships and know-how are the keys whereas, in the second, patent coverage is vital, since it effectively creates a monopoly for a period.

With increasing international competitiveness, many companies want to maintain and concentrate on their technical and Intellectual Property Rights (IPR) strengths and do not wish to be embroiled in the logistical pressures of international business. Their formula is to create a relatively sound home company which has a strong IPR portfolio, as well as control of its domestic market. The imaginative exploitation of these strengths internationally through chosen partners is very much the order of the day.

Tomorrow's successful technology company is therefore likely to have much of its activity and value tied up in its IPR portfolio, allied to intelligent marketing, distribution and manufacturing arrangements. Alternatively, it may concentrate on providing an overall service or systems solution to a customer's needs, around its base product or technology, and buy-in from elsewhere the other products required in the solution. Both types of company can be highly profitable and are also able to remain flexible and light on their feet, which are great assets in a fast-changing world with ever-increasing international competition.

From an investment standpoint, many people believe that if they back exciting and leading-edge technology, the company involved will be a success and will make them a great deal of money. The reality is often very different since products, however advanced and clever the technology on which they are based, will not sell if they are not carefully matched to market needs. This is usually because either they do not have a specific enough commercial application, with an early pay-back to the customer of the cost involved, or that they are too early for the market which is not ready to take advantage of what they have to offer. Tactics and timing are, therefore, very important in launching a new product on the market, if it is to be a commercial success.

SEVEN

ENTREPRENEURS, MANAGERS AND DIRECTORS

ENTREPRENEURS are a rare breed who are strong on intuition and deductive reasoning and whose instincts lead them to a solution in advance of facts and proof, along the lines of Aristarchus deducing that the earth revolved around the sun 1,900 years before Galileo enabled it to be proved, as referred to earlier. The Atomists, who deduced that the Universe is made up of atoms at about the same time, are another amazing example, as is Thales of Miletus who is reported to have accurately predicted the year of the first recorded eclipse of 585 BC.

The ability of entrepreneurs to be certain of the right path ahead is an advantage in a start-up situation but can be a double-edged sword in a larger company, unless they are underpinned by good management and are prepared to adapt their ways. The old adage that a good chief executive makes his decisions instinctively, and uses his training to convince his colleagues, has some truth in it.

Of course, intuition and instinct have their limitations and should, wherever possible, be backed by factual proof, although the big decisions usually have a judgement gap to jump, since facts are often limited. An example is the creation of a new market, often referred to as missionary marketing, where no past statistics are available.

Successful entrepreneurs usually combine a positive, generous side with a negative, protective one, rather like a Jekyll and Hyde combination. The first enables them to take bold, imaginative steps with a vision that inspires them and their colleagues, whilst the second ensures that they exploit opportunities commercially and are able to fend off threats.

In my opinion, entrepreneurs are born and cannot be created, despite numerous books, business school efforts and government incentives, which seek to produce them from the general population. Many true entrepreneurs started with financial deprivation or lost a parent early, which gave them a powerful mix of financial insecurity and enforced self-reliance. The first acts as a spur to commercial success and the second enables them to be at ease in standing on their own feet, since starting and running a company can be a lonely pastime.

Entrepreneurs gravitate towards setting up their own businesses, through a need to express themselves, and to achieve operating freedom. People who are not natural entrepreneurs and without a burning desire to fulfil a vision, should not set up a company for the sake of it or because they feel that they ought to, since they are unlikely to succeed. Instead, they should concentrate on applying their strengths in other roles.

Entrepreneurs are as fallible as any other breed and can become seduced by success which is, in many ways, even more dangerous than failure. It is said that 'the only good experience is bad experience' since people learn from their setbacks or failures and are not then subject to flattery or delusions of grandeur. Inflated egos, complacency or arrogance are all bad signs from an investment standpoint and usually lead to disaster.

Entrepreneurs are very loyal and reciprocative if well treated but never forget an injury, another example of the Jekyll and Hyde trait mentioned earlier. They like their own way and sometimes need standing up to but, if you do, you had better be right. On one Board that I was a member of, if you argued and won a point with the founder, it was never mentioned again, whereas if proved wrong, it was brought up with great regularity!

Entrepreneurs are not initially motivated by money but by the intoxicating power of a new idea, in line with Victor Hugo's belief in the limitless power of an idea whose time has come. They want to fulfil a dream in their own mind, want to enjoy the chase of achieving it and want their efforts to be successful, which, in a private enterprise situation, means profit.

This combination of vision, challenge and success is known in the US as 'the gamesman approach' which is why many good sportsmen make excellent executives. Sportsmen tend to be competitive and know that they have to play well to win.

The successful fulfilment of their ambitions often results in entrepreneurs achieving wealth beyond their wildest dreams but the good ones are not corrupted by the money, even though their descendants may be. There are many examples of the Dutch adage of 'clogs to clogs in three generations'.

The dictum of strategy without successful execution being a waste of time, as mentioned earlier, is relevant to good entrepreneurs and to good managers, both of whom must be able to get things done. Managers, who become an increasingly essential component of executive resources as the company expands in size, are a less individualistic breed than entrepreneurs but the effective ones are reliable, team based and able to get the detail right.

Managers rely more heavily on analysis than entrepreneurs and, as the business grows, there is more to analyse. In a successful enterprise, the right balance between an entrepreneur and his supporting managers is vital with, ideally, their different strengths complementing each other. For a business to continue to grow without disruption, every effort should be made to foster and retain this balance for as long as possible.

Balance within a management team is also very important and all the key functions of a company should be properly represented, with different industries requiring different biases, although finance is always important. New companies are normally driven at the outset from the marketing or product end but, as they grow, are increasingly dependent on the harnessing and management of resources.

Good Chief Executive or Operating Officers are often those who have moved beyond their original discipline and, in the process, have become emancipated from it. It is sometimes said that second-class professionals become managers because people who are not enthralled and captivated by their own speciality, move out of it to take on a more general and wider role. If you are an Albert Einstein, you stick to science!

Two essential lessons for an entrepreneur are first, never to be talked out of his or her instincts, particularly by people who claim to be certain that they are right, and second, only to give to and work with people who reciprocate. Reciprocation is the key to all good relationships and to the building of a strong team.

I have seen more 'organisation men' ruin a business by too much management method than entrepreneurs do so with too little. However, the key is to have a complementary blend of entrepreneurial and management resources and talent, as referred to earlier. The bigger a company gets, the more it is dependent on sound management and method, albeit applied in a commercial manner suited to the company's successful style of operation.

Board role and structure is an important subject in this context and is more fully covered in a paper which I wrote some years ago, included as Appendix III, since much of it is still relevant. In the UK, Boards normally comprise a mix of executive and non-executive representation, with each executive having to play a different role as a director, to their day-to-day one. One man is supposed to have insisted on being called by a different name at Board meetings in order to remind himself of the difference.

The Chairman, who increasingly in public companies is part-time, has a vital role to play to lead the Board, co-ordinate its disparate components and ensure its effective running. Classically, a good entrepreneur will gravitate towards this role, ideally supported by an excellent Chief Executive Officer (CEO) or Chief Operating Officer (COO) and a strong Chief Financial Officer (CFO), with the balance between the three roles being vital.

In situations in which the entrepreneur is no longer in the company and the team is management centred, the Chairman is usually non-executive with a professional background, such as accountancy or law. His role in such situations is more reactive and related to finance, as in a financial holding company, or to law, with the ever-increasing demands of corporate governance.

Outside non-executive directors have an important role to play in contributing to a Board's dialogue and success and, in particular, they need to challenge the company's plans and monitor its executive team. Getting hold of good non-executive directors who can genuinely contribute to a company's development is, however, easier said than done, since the best people are already heavily engaged in commercial activity and are loathe to take on added liability and corporate governance exposure. The increased remuneration which is now being paid to non-executive directors will, however, be of help in this process.

Ideally, for a young growth company, a Board should be made up of two-thirds executive and one-third non-executive directors, and should have a balance of skills covering the business, its resources and finance. As a company grows, and particularly in the US, the non-executive representation on a Board increases and often reverses the ratio of two-thirds to one-third.

In most public companies, non-executives would have formal roles as respective chairmen of the Audit, Nominations and Remuneration Committees but, in a venture capital situation, the issue will be handled more informally, and often more effectively, because there is less emphasis on form and more on substance. Small private companies need to retain their commercial flair and be fast-moving, if they are to survive, and too much method can strangle them.

Boards should meet physically on a regular basis, with telephone or video-conference meetings in between, with the latter two categories becoming increasingly relevant, due to the costs, duration and frustrations of air travel. In all of these Board meetings, the preparation of relevant documents in good time is vital to their successful execution and their effective contribution to the company.

Shareholder relationships are equally vital and formal reporting, even in a private company, should comprise Interim and Final Accounts, with an Annual Meeting, as a required minimum. Subject to insider trading rules, information content and dialogue between these formal events is also important, so that shareholders feel that they are being kept up to speed with major developments and are not subject to nasty surprises.

Building a new company is like finding one's way through a dangerous jungle, albeit a commercial one, and a company's top management and Board must combine professional competence with commercial flair. At all stages of a company's development, they must continue to be street-wise, combining clear direction to find the right path with an alertness to look out for the tigers behind the trees.

EIGHT

THE MANAGEMENT
OF RESOURCES

W ITHIN the concept of building international niche businesses which have global ambitions but are focused on
a narrow range of products and services, it is important
to concentrate resources on the essential activities for these businesses and to use them to maximum effect. This will often mean
concentrating on final assembly and sub-contracting out all, or
the bulk of component supply, thus enabling the business in
question to be light on its feet and able to respond quickly to
rapid changes in markets and economic conditions.

In this framework, it will be important to get the big things
right in the harnessing and use of resources, such as the selection,
training and motivation of staff, and so put less emphasis on the
traditional productivity aids of value analysis and work study,
although these will still have their place in the component and
sub-assembly suppliers.

Staff are, for healthcare and technology businesses, usually the
most important and expensive item and great care needs to be
taken to ensure that the right balance and calibre of people are
employed in every function of the business, not least on the technical front where product development and design are critical in
these sectors. Although good people are hard to find, they are
worth searching for, since they can make the difference between
success and failure in a business.

Once a cadre of quality staff has been assembled, it is important that they should have a clear idea of the company's
strategy and of their part in it. There is no substitute for a well
written policy document, kept up-to-date and communicated to
them by their top management, so that everyone in the group is

inspired by the same message and encouraged to co-operate together in order to achieve the desired aims. This is particularly relevant in groups which are geographically dispersed.

Assuming that this essential communication has been achieved, then management effort should be concentrated on ensuring that staff receive regular training, to assist them in their defined tasks, and given helpful reviews that applaud their achievements and make them aware of areas where their performance can be improved. It is important that such reviews should be carried out diplomatically, particularly in the UK where people are, in general, sensitive to any implied criticism.

In the US, staff are usually more responsive to constructive proposals for enhancement, since one of the great American strengths is a heavy emphasis on self-improvement. They are also more robust at dealing with the fall-out of success and failure, although sometimes this can be taken too far as with 'the steak and beans dinner', in which, at the end of the year, the winning sales team eats steak and the losing one beans!

While a lot of communication to and between staff can be done over the telephone and electronically, there is no substitute for some physical contact, particularly in international groups with different countries, races and cultures. One way of achieving this is for Board meetings to be held, say once a year, at different sites so that a company's directors, management and staff have sufficient personal contact.

Another way is to hold an annual sales conference for the company and to invite key management and staff to attend. This worked well in one US company of which I was Chairman and it fell to me each year to give a 'State of the Nation' address in a relaxed setting and in a light-hearted manner. After fifteen years and out of jokes, I felt that I needed a rest and was having a bath at home, congratulating myself on my decision to take a break, when the telephone rang and it was the President saying that he had the whole company assembled and in need of a bit of light relief.

Like Archimedes, I sought inspiration from the water and told them the old chestnut about three men, with poor hearing, on a train. When this pulls into a station, one says 'Is this Wembley?', the second says 'No, it's Thursday' and the third says 'So am I, let's go and have a drink!' The company was in the hearing health field so the enforced attempt at instant humour was relevant, although it rightly had to be presented and viewed in a sympathetic light, since the company was deeply committed to providing products for hearing improvement.

Turning to resources other than staff, it is vital that investment should be concentrated on the equipment that a company requires to carry out its essential functions. Proper procedures should be in place to evaluate such capital investments and key staff, who will be operating the equipment, should be fully involved in the process. Once equipment has been purchased, it should be well maintained and kept for as long as practical. It is often better, as with motor cars, to have a quality machine for a long time than to keep chopping and changing, with all the disruption and expense that the latter involves.

Thirdly, property, the other key resource, is normally leasehold for a young company in order to give it flexibility and free up capital which can achieve superior earnings in the business. I am not against ownership of freeholds, via a mortgage, once things have settled down, but property assets should be subordinate to trading ones in a growth business.

The location of property can be important, particularly to serve customers and to help attract the right people into the business. This is why so many technology companies flourish in the environs of science-based universities, such as Cambridge in the UK and Stanford in the US.

Accountants often make good resource managers, when they are sensitive to people, since they are used to controlling costs and getting the best out of resources. In general, the aim should be to have a plant which meets the needs of the company and looks neat and tidy, both to give a good impression to customers and suppliers and to give staff a pride in their activities.

NINE

FINANCIAL PHILOSOPHY AND CONTROL

ABOUT 2,000 years ago, Horace, the Roman poet, wrote 'By fair means if you can but, by any means, make money'. He would probably be criticised in today's society for encouraging greed and unscrupulousness, even though, presumably, he was only trying to emphasise the importance of the bottom line, or whatever it was called in those days.

The key financial criteria in today's private enterprise system, which are the measures of a venture's success are profitability, cash flow and net assets. Profitability, usually expressed as profit before tax, reflects the current trading health of a corporation; it is closely linked to cash flow which, like the blood supply of a human body, enables the latter to work effectively. Net assets represents the value that has been built up in a business, usually over a number of years, from original capital injections and the subsequent accumulation of non-distributed after-tax profits.

For growth businesses, particularly in the US, Revenue Growth is also viewed as very important in measuring the success of a business and calculating its value. There is logic in this but only if such growth produces satisfactory results for the three criteria specified above. It is a salutary fact that nine out of ten businesses which go bust, do so by over-trading, which essentially means too much revenue expansion at too low profit margins. This usually has disastrous effects on cash flow and the company in question runs quickly out of money.

Like such companies, many people are better at spending money than making it, particularly in today's society where borrowing is so cheap and so easy to come by. In the end, though, financial imprudence ends in tears, as highlighted by Mr Micawber's classic definition in David Copperfield of 'happiness being income greater than expenditure and unhappiness being income less than expenditure'.

People are born with attributes of frugality or spendthriftness and never really change in their attitude to money, unless they have a major disaster or near-disaster which produces a Damascene conversion. Even that only occurs with a fortunate few, since, for the majority, the cycles of financial behaviour repeat themselves.

On the other hand, people who have a similar and sensible attitude to money can work easily together and will normally be able to sort out all their other problems. People who are unwise with money, will conversely create major problems for themselves and their partners, with financial incompatibility and insecurity being a, if not the most, common factor in the breakdown of business relationships and marriages.

In a venture capital situation, it is vital that entrepreneurs and managers have the right attitude to money and are focused on profits, cash flow and net assets, with the aim of building up a strong balance sheet for their company. Many people give lip service to these aims but are incapable of the discipline and rigorousness required to achieve them. They are, in many ways, the most dangerous executives because, by telling investors and shareholders what they want to hear, they lull them into a false sense of security. This leads to a rude awakening when the reality surfaces.

Many executives also make excuses for their lack of financial performance and sometimes argue that, if they had had more investment, they would have been more successful. Such attitudes and excuses are unproductive and self-defeating, since their owners will never learn and improve. There is no disgrace in failure, if one has tried as hard as possible to prevent it, but there is every disgrace in not learning from one's failure, and then repeating it.

Whatever the management philosophy in a venture capital situation, it is vital that tight financial control and monitoring should be exercised; otherwise the Board of a company will not have its finger on the pulse and is likely to receive a nasty shock at some stage. The old Russian proverb 'Trust but Verify' is appropriate to financial control, as is the dictum that 'delegation, without monitoring, is abdication'.

If too much financial latitude is given to an executive or an executive team, the Board is not properly fulfilling its obligation of monitoring a business and, at the same time, is putting temptation into the hands of individuals who can be all too fallible in such a situation. When things go wrong, it then has the invidious task of suspending the person or persons involved while it investigates and, depending on the outcome of its research, taking punitive action which can be unpleasant for all concerned. A carefully structured and spelt out system of financial delegation and control can therefore save a lot of heartache and wasted time.

It is vital, therefore, to have a tight system of financial control so that the Board and its management know what is happening in the business, with a view to being able to take early action to remedy problems. Such a system would normally comprise a properly worked out budget for the year, monthly management accounts and bi-annual financial accounts which, in the UK, would be audited, although, in the US, this is not compulsory for private companies. Longer-term financial plans, based on the company's business plan, would also normally be prepared in order to plan investment and to deal with questions, on a separate front, from financial analysts and investors, particularly in a public company context.

Companies in trouble need, conversely, very short-term financial reports, of which the most important is cash flow; these can be daily or weekly, coupled to a rolling cash flow forecast for six to twelve months ahead. Cynics say that the last thing that a bad company needs is to have a good accounting system put in, since it will show, for the first time, the harsh reality of the situation and will provide the evidence for a bank or other creditor to foreclose.

For successful companies, the key to good profits and cash flow is to have a focused market and product strategy which yields good margins on relatively low overheads. It is only when expansion in turnover is over 40% per annum that cash flow becomes negative for such companies, and that is for the entirely positive reason of funding increased working capital, which is not normally a problem to finance. Conversely, firms which have a wide market and product base, relatively low margins and high overheads, are usually cash-negative from the outset and are very vulnerable to downturns in the market or other adverse conditions.

Ten

Financing and Its Structures

ENTURE capital, as defined earlier, is about getting a high
return on an investment which normally means investing
in high growth companies and sectors. The most appropriate financial instrument for this is ordinary shares or common stock which will help, first, the company's cash flow and growth, and secondly, will give the investor a substantially better return than geared equity, if things go according to plan.

The other point about ordinary shares or common stock is that they put the venture capital investor in the same position as a company's entrepreneur and managers, and this helps to cement the relationship and financial partnership, since everyone is on the same side and in the same boat. They also leave the company open to sensible borrowing, as and when this looks desirable or necessary, either to exploit commercial opportunities, such as to help finance an acquisition, or to deal with a temporary hiccup in business.

Start-ups of any kind should not be geared, as they have enough risks and cash flow pressures of their own, without these being compounded by borrowing. On the other hand, for more mature companies with only moderate growth, it often makes sense for venture capital investors to bring in a package of equity and redeemable shares or debentures, coupled with reasonable bank borrowing. Even in these situations, however, the approach should be conservative and gearing limited.

Sometimes, in a situation in which there is a wide difference in valuation between a company and prospective investors, a convertible debenture or preferred share has relevance and is the only way in which this difference can be bridged. It is more applicable to a later-stage growth company rather than an early-stage one and has particular relevance to a pre-IPO financing, with convertibility set at a discount to the ultimate float price.

The aim in financing venture capital investments should be to keep things as simple as possible, and orientated to the needs of the company. On the same basis as Alfred Sloan's famous saying that 'what is good for General Motors is good for America', simple and logical structures more often make money than complicated ones, imposed to meet the supposed needs of shareholders, and, in the end, better serve the interests of these shareholders.

On the same basis, tax avoidance or minimisation schemes are not good news for venture capital investments, since they also put the cart before the horse. This is one of the reasons that so many government sponsored initiatives founder.

Sight must not be lost of the fact that good venture capital investments have so much upside that financing and its structures should seek to facilitate and enhance their growth and should not be preoccupied with protecting investors' rights in the event of a disaster. In many venture capital investments, particularly in early-stage ones, there is nothing to argue about in such an event and, psychologically, it creates the wrong climate for a growth situation, with 'the wish often being father to the thought'.

Similarly, the gain on a good venture capital investment will dwarf any short-term tax advantage and other things which people worry about, such as currency movements. This does not mean, of course, that steps should not be taken to minimise tax or cover currency risks, within the framework of a logically based financing scheme, arranged predominantly for the company's benefit.

Another factor which is important in arranging financing is the valuation of the company, and here a reasonable compromise needs to be struck between the interests of the entrepreneur and those of the venture capital investor since, following a deal, they will have to work closely together for a period of up to, say, seven years. Looking back on an investment, like looking back on a house purchase years later, it is amazing how unimportant the original price appears in relation to the exit value, even though, at the time, it seemed of vital significance.

Share options and warrants have a place in capital structures but should be used sensibly in situations, for instance, where they are issued in order to give management and key staff a stake in the business and to motivate them to help develop it successfully. Both instruments should, however, be carefully rationed and controlled, and issued at a price that reflects the current value of the business, so that the rewards derived from them are earned through its genuine enhancement.

Options and warrants are particularly relevant where a company's capital base is made up entirely of ordinary shares or common stock since, as a company progresses, they are the only way in which staff can be brought into the equity on reasonable terms. Where leveraging exists, they are not so necessary, certainly at the outset, since management can move into the ordinary shares without having to contribute to the debt, which often makes up a large part of the initial capitalisation.

Eleven

Start-Ups

T HE BEST start-ups comprise a big idea, a lot of effort from a committed entrepreneur and a small amount of money. The disciplines learnt in starting up a company from scratch are never forgotten, like checking the cash position every day, and the salient fact for an entrepreneur is that he has to get things done himself, since there is no one else to do it. This is one of the reasons why many large company executives are out of their element in a young company because they are used to having things done for them by a substantial team.

Start-ups or early-stage investments that I have been personally involved in are Thompson Clive which had an initial capitalisation of £100, effectively being a venture capital organisation without any capital at the outset, Pantheon Holdings which began on nominal capital of £50,000 and a loan facility of about £200,000 that was never used and, now, Solon Ventures which has been launched with an initial capital of £50,000 in order to meet FSA requirements. In each case, the axiom of 'think big and act small' was applied, which is a good rule for such situations.

A start-up can be market or concept led in which the opportunity is clearly identified, either as a replacement product sale or involving the creation of a new market which is often known as missionary marketing. Or it can be product led, where a technological breakthrough creates many opportunities, and the problem is to prioritise them and make sure that the technology and its associated products are applied in a commercial way.

Behind these market and product initiatives, there must be a committed entrepreneur who is infused with the opportunities offered and is determined to exploit them. The concept and the entrepreneur come a joint first in terms of importance in a start-up and the money, or what there is of it, a poor third.

41

Start-ups in the US have a different philosophy and back a new market or product concept with a large amount of money which can be relevant in, say, a biotechnology situation. However, new ventures there are sometimes flooded with too much money which can be counterproductive in the same way as over-fertilising a garden or passing on too much money to young people, which can corrupt them and sap their initiative.

The US investment world can afford to take an aggressive financial attitude to start-ups because new companies can be built quickly to significant size in the domestic economy and large companies are more prepared to snap them up earlier for good prices than in Europe, thus enabling the gamble to be worthwhile. The US also has a much greater availability of capital, both from private individuals and from institutions.

Attitudes in the US are conducive to having a go, since failure is not viewed as a disaster as it is in the UK, where people take the stigma of a major one with them to their grave. In the US, on the other hand, the response is often 'bad luck, have another go'. In Japan, failure is not often identified with an individual because most decisions are taken on a group basis.

Start-ups rely heavily on intuition and logic, as well as a good sense of timing, since many great ideas have come to grief by being applied too early to the market. That is why entrepreneurs need to be certain, through their instincts, that they are right, even though everyone may tell them that they are wrong. In my case in 1977, in my first start-up, I had a letter from a friend saying 'I hear that you are involved in launching a new company; what a brave decision, I hope that you do not live to regret it.'

In start-ups, as discussed earlier, 75% of reading a new market or product opportunity is instinct or intuition and 25% is based on fact, which is often severely limited in such situations. This compares to a 50:50 intuition to fact split in the judgement of people, and 25:75 in making a financial judgement of a company.

The ideal person to start up a company in the healthcare or technology markets is someone with a relevant scientific training and a natural commercial flair. He can be helped to develop and build the business by a good venture capital partner but only if he fully understands, and is inspired by the scientific or technical ideas that he is selling.

Start-ups should not be geared, as stated earlier, and should be run in a manner to make them profitable and cash self-sufficient as soon as possible. Where sizeable start-up funds are required, they should be provided in one round financings, with the aim of making the company stand on its own feet as soon as possible. Endless refinancings from weakness are bad news for investors, and not good for the ethos of the company.

New biotechnology companies are often set up with substantial funding, albeit called down in a series of tranches. They usually have a long incubation period of up to ten years or more where the company has to get its products through Phases I–III of the regulatory process. They tend to be known as high capitalisation start-ups and, although an established brand of venture capital, they are not often practised by me, as I prefer to try to make money without high risk.

University spin-offs of technology are another specialised brand of venture capital which are growing in importance as universities become increasingly keen, in the face of reduced government funding, to exploit their technological assets. A fund concentrating entirely on such spin-offs is difficult to make a commercial success of, as all the ventures are high risk, and a mixed portfolio is a better way to handle the opportunities, since risk to reward ratios are more balanced.

Often the biggest successes are ultimately those with the smallest initial capitalisations, certainly from an internal rate of return (IRR) standpoint. For this reason, I do not have a minimum size of investment when looking at an opportunity, unlike most people in the industry who are concerned with putting substantial sums to work.

In looking at a start-up or first-stage financing from an investment standpoint, close attention must be paid to the company's existing customers because often it will be dependent on one or two of them, the loss of which would have a very detrimental effect on the business. Sometimes the company may have no revenue at all and, in these circumstances, the likelihood of it achieving early sales to prospective customers is equally, if not more, important. It is vital that such first-stage companies should move into profitability early and not develop a dependency culture of making losses and needing continual refinancing.

The evaluation of an entrepreneur in a first-stage financing is usually the key to an investment since the company's progress will initially be, almost entirely, in his or her hands. The evaluation should look for vision, commitment, persuasiveness, drive, frugality and trustworthiness.

Initially, financial progress will largely depend upon the company's ability to produce sales and keep overheads down, with the bootstrapping approach being the ideal one. Where more substantial expenditure is necessary at the outset, the money should be carefully husbanded by the entrepreneur, since the company is unlikely to be able to afford a full-time Finance Director at this stage.

The exit options for a first-stage business are not usually the priority, since success in the investment will open up several alternatives. It is also premature to think of an exit some years ahead before the business has been established, although it is more relevant in the US where early acquisition of young companies is more prevalent.

TWELVE

SECOND-STAGE FINANCINGS

SECOND-STAGE financings arise when a business with a product has been established and ideally enough turnover has been created in its home market to enable it to reach or be close to profitability. The key for a company at that stage is to have a clear marketing plan showing how the lead product can be sold to a wider market, which may involve some selling overseas, and how further products can be developed for sale to existing markets. This involves a combination of market and product development as set out in the matrix below:

1 Existing Markets Existing Products	**2** New Markets Existing Products
3 Existing Markets New Products	**4** New Markets New Products

The first box of the matrix shows a company's current situation, the next two cover in turn market and product development, which are respectively low and medium risk, and the last represents diversification, which is high risk, and often attempted through acquisition.

The management team will need to expand to cope with and help achieve the anticipated expansion, and the key functions at this stage are often marketing and finance. In this, a focused strategy for the company is important as it is easier and safer to achieve on a narrow front on the Blitzkrieg principle of applying overwhelming force to an opportunity which, in military terms, is usually an opponent's weakness. In the industrial field, it means having a good but narrow product range and selling it to a clearly identified market, with the aims of achieving high margins.

Often a company's management will go through a 'SWOT' analysis in defining its strategy. This involves clearly identifying its strengths and weaknesses on the one hand and market opportunities and threats on the other. Its strategy will normally then involve applying its strengths to the market opportunities in a positive way and, at the same time, taking steps to rectify weaknesses and counter market threats.

Second-stage financings require more finance than start-ups, which is a plus since they are less risky and the rewards are more defined. There should be a clear plan of what the money is needed for and of the returns anticipated, although the same principle of not over-financing should be applied. This is, however, a very real risk, since many private equity companies manage large funds and want to put more of it to work than the situation warrants, often with unfortunate results.

Second-stage financings are an exciting stage in a company's life and can be likened to adolescent years where the venture capitalist needs to provide good supportive help in order to bring the company to maturity and enable it to stand on its own feet. Done properly, such financings can be very profitable and provide the foundation for a company's future growth and continued success; they are usually also the bedrock of a good venture capital portfolio.

The investment evaluation for a second-stage financing will need to look closely at the existing customer base, since there is still likely to be some dependency on a few customers with a large share of turnover. The loss of a big account, after an investment, can often be a major embarrassment to the business and can set its progress back a long way.

Assuming that the existing customer base is sound, equal attention must be given to the company's prospects in its domestic market. Building on its domestic base will enhance the company's stability and enable it to strike out into the international market from strength, assuming that good opportunities are in it. There need to be good prospects internationally for a UK or Continental business, otherwise it will not be able to achieve adequate organic expansion, since domestic markets are relatively small in Europe.

Moving on to people, the entrepreneur will continue to be very important since he is still likely to be playing a 'hands-on' role. However, the potential investor must be satisfied that he is capable of delegating and building up an executive team to support his efforts.

One or two building bricks of this team should be in place and be seen to be working efficiently. Some entrepreneurs find it difficult to develop harmonious and complementary relationships with managers, and end up constantly changing their subordinates, which is very disruptive to a business and gives it little management stability or continuity.

Turning to finance, the company is likely to have reached a stage where it has a full-time Finance Director and proper systems of financial control. If this is not the case, the introduction of these financial desiderata should be a condition of the investment.

On exits, the company is likely to have the option of either a flotation or trade sale, depending on progress and the aspirations of its staff. The matter does not need to be decided at the point of investment but will evolve over the years ahead, with the venture capitalist assisting in the right decision being reached at the appropriate time.

Thirteen

Third-Stage Financings

THIRD-STAGE financings follow on from the second-stage of a company's development and usually involve it moving from a national to an international base. This process is a complicated one and requires a good understanding of the size and demands of different world markets and an appreciation of their cultures, behavioural patterns, languages, ethics and legal and tax systems.

As stated earlier, many European companies come to grief in selling to the large US market and, vice-versa, many US companies also find that their big company or country model does not fit the fragmented European market. Maybe the situation will change in due course, but at the moment, the Single European Market is not a reality and is unlikely to become one in the foreseeable future.

The process of moving to be an international company continues to require a clearly focused strategy, expressed through a business plan, and should be led by organic growth. Tactical acquisitions, aimed at accelerating market and product development, can, however, be helpful where they are within the strategy and can be easily absorbed into the mainstream culture, which probably means that they have to be relatively small in relation to the base business. Another benefit of small, tactical acquisitions is that, if they fail, their impact on the whole company is limited, which is not always the case with large acquisitions.

The process of internationalising a business will require consideration being given to appointing exclusive or non-exclusive distributors, setting up overseas subsidiaries, joint ventures with other companies or making acquisitions. The main thrust of such efforts should be to create an international niche business and, in the process, it is vital to combine a wide market coverage with a narrow product range, so that flexibility can be retained in a fast-moving world, with the aim no longer being to become a large company, long on resources and muscle power.

Increasingly, the model for an international niche business is for a company to concentrate on keeping control of its product range and associated IPR and, perhaps, of its domestic market. In order to maintain flexibility and reduce investment exposure and risks, it may well wish to exploit the potential of overseas markets and new market sectors through carefully selected partners which it influences but does not control.

Third-stage financings, aimed at creating international niche businesses, provide the dream ticket for the investor of high reward and low risk, if done properly. They are particularly important in the UK, where companies cannot become big organically without being international. A venture capitalist who can genuinely help this process, is worth his weight in gold and deserves the rewards, in this and other elements, which a successful investment brings.

From an investment standpoint, the first thing to evaluate on a third-stage financing is the quality and strength of the existing business, since a stable base is vital to any plans for international expansion. Once this has been determined, attention should be focused on the overseas market potential of the company's products and technologies and the way in which they can be best exploited, in essence checking its strategy, assuming that it has one.

In the wake of this evaluation, the would-be investor needs to be satisfied that the company's management is good enough, and has a sufficient balance and depth, to capitalise on the potential which is available. All aspects of management are likely to be tested by the task of building an international business, ranging from the strategic functions of market and financial planning through to the tactical support needed to be given by departmental functions such as development and production. All of this endeavour needs to be brought to bear without loss of momentum to the base business, so having strength and depth in management and resources is vital to a successful outcome.

Assuming that the strategic imperatives and management

capabilities match up, it is important that sufficient thought is given to the way in which the international business will be controlled, including the monitoring of any overseas subsidiaries, joint ventures or trading partners who are integral to the plans. It is also important that sufficient thought is given, and research done, on those aspects of overseas trading which are going to affect the success of the international expansion of the business, such as the legal and tax regimes of the countries involved.

Because third-stage financings tend to be associated with businesses which are relatively large and becoming more complicated internationally, the exit options need to be carefully thought through, since they are likely to be fewer. In most cases, the preferred route will be to go for a float down the road, since the company is likely to be a self-sufficient entity with a balance of growth and spread internationally. Once it has proved itself and its formula in public markets it may, of course, attract attention from a larger company, whose profile and objectives it fits.

FOURTEEN

TURNROUNDS

T HE SKILLS of turnround are important in venture capital, either when correcting a substantial investment which has gone wrong or sometimes in taking advantage of the opportunity offered by a company in trouble, either in the private or public domain. When the opportunity is a public company, it is usually desirable to privatise the company in order to take it out of the public spotlight whilst applying the appropriate remedies. These usually comprise pruning out any unprofitable product lines (assuming that reasonable product cost information is available), cutting back on non-essential staff, reducing unproductive overheads (particularly at head office), and selling off or closing loss-making businesses at whatever value can be got.

The aim of these actions is to create higher margin turnover with a lower overhead weighting, and then to allow the good business to come through and develop, with beneficial profit and cash flow results. Improving cash flow is the key to most company doctoring, since it enables the company to stem the flow of cash out and ultimately to become self-financing.

Often the person who leads the company doctoring is financially orientated and, of necessity, short-term in his thrust, since the objective is to stay alive. He is not usually the right person to expand the residual business, since this process requires a positive and longer-term business development skill, with an emphasis on marketing and strategy.

Signs of a company heading for trouble include too wide a product base, an excess of staff, complacency and arrogance in the management inviting hubris, and an over-prestigious head office confirming the old Turkish proverb that 'when the house is finished, death enters'. Other signs are high profile awards, personalised number plates on executive cars (particularly when they are expensive), the opening of a new factory by a leading politician and other ego-enhancing events. Inflated egos are a major disadvantage in a company, since they tend to divert management from seeking the right answer to a problem and, instead, make individuals more interested in being seen to be the person providing the answer. They are a big turn-off or sell sign for an investment.

There is no substitute for getting rid of the top management who have created the problems in a company in trouble, since they will be psychologically resistant to the steps required to rectify the situation. On the other hand, there will usually be good people in the tier below who will be vital in achieving the turnround and who can flourish in a different environment.

Turnrounds in the US are somewhat easier than in the UK because employment laws are less protective and attitudes more responsive to necessary change. On the Continent, they are conversely even more difficult than here, with Belgium and France being notorious in that respect, due to their social legislation.

The key investment decision, when looking at a turnround, is whether the company can be moved into profitability in a reasonable time-frame of no more than one to two years and how much effort and money the process is likely to involve. It is very easy to underestimate both of these aspects in a turnround and to become trapped in an untenable situation.

Assuming that a turnround in a reasonable time-frame can be achieved, the company should only be of interest to a venture capitalist if it can be used as a building brick for further development and expansion. In essence, the real job starts once the turnround has been effected.

A good turnround specialist or company doctor will have to apply the required medicine himself initially, and he is likely to be nicely surprised by some things in the company but equally disappointed by others, which he will need to eradicate or correct. Once a turnround has been successfully achieved, he will then need to bring in permanent management suited to the long-term development of the business, effectively doing himself out of a job in the process, unless he takes on a part-time role.

The company will need to have a strong financial function and effective financial controls established during the turnround. It should be run tightly for profit and cash flow thereafter.

With regard to exit options, a company can either be floated or refloated, assuming that it either is, or has become, a private company. Alternatively, it is often bid for by a prospective suitor, once the turnround medicine has been effectively applied, and the heat has been taken out of the situation. A well-timed bid in these circumstances is hard to counter, since the price being offered usually seems good in relation to historic performance.

FIFTEEN

STRATEGIC AND OTHER ALLIANCES

As a business grows, strategic alliances become very important since they give a small company added clout in a competitive international world, without saddling it with permanent overheads. Just as the aim is to concentrate on core activities that the business does well, other companies have the same idea and welcome off-loading specialist activities that they would be unlikely to be able to keep up-to-date with.

Good strategic alliances give stability to a small company and give it credibility in going for large and often international contracts which would be difficult for it on its own. The health-care industry is ideally suited for such arrangements as it is dominated by a number of large, international pharmaceutical majors who are very happy to have strategic alliances with smaller biotechnology and clinical trials companies, to name but two examples. Both sides usually benefit from this arrangement which can also be a precursor to a full integration, if desirable and desired.

Another example in the technology sector might be a software company with a high emphasis on product design and development, which wants to concentrate on building a strong IPR portfolio for its business. In these circumstances, it may wish to remain technically driven and to off-load the marketing responsibility and costs for its products, either to a big company with strong distribution capability, or to parallel marketing companies which it helps to set up in different parts of the world, financed by local sources.

There is no need anymore to own 100% of all aspects of an international business and often the better answer is to concentrate on the key functions which a company has leadership in and to rely on other people for the exploitation of these strengths, certainly in far-flung international markets. As long as sensible fall-back arrangements are in place, if such an alliance does not work out, control of IPR can be maintained, with little cost exposure.

As mentioned, strategic alliances generally exist between a large company and a small one, since the former is able to take a long-term view and to give long-term comfort to both sides. Sometimes they will involve the large company taking a stake in the small one, more from a protective than a predatory stance, and this can provide added stability to the situation as well as being a useful form of supplementary funding for the small one. Where such arrangements exist, it is important that it can be unwound relatively easily, following the precept of 'planning for the worst, but then going for the best'.

Other alliances, usually between companies of similar size, can involve companies selling each other's products reciprocally, where they are approaching the same customer base, or one company selling another's products on a more traditional agency or distributor basis. In all such situations, it is vital that the industrial logic should be thought through, that the chemistry and trust between the two companies should be good and that both sides should reap a fair reward from the arrangement. Reciprocity is the key to continuing success in a relationship.

Next, there are the alliances which exist between a product company and a supplier. These normally arise where specialist technology or equipment is involved, and can range from the buying-in of a key component to the contracting out of full manufacture where, for instance, high levels of cleanliness or sterilisation are required, as in the pharmaceutical industry. Such alliances make sense where both parties need the assurance of continuing business in order to make a success of niche areas but they should be entered into judiciously, as they can create dependencies and reduce the competitive market pressures that normally exist between buyers and suppliers.

The alliances discussed are a good way to take a small company forward without burdening it with added investment pressures. Indeed, some alliances provide the basis for investment into the company from a trading partner if this is desirable and does not constrain its freedom of manoeuvre and operation. An exception to this could be a joint venture with an equal partner where both sides need to put up similar sums of money to get the joint venture off the ground.

An investment relationship with a partner can enhance or complicate a company's exit options, depending on the partner and the exit route chosen. In the main, a float is best achieved when a company is a truly independent entity, from a shareholder point of view, whereas a trade sale could be enhanced by having an equity partner with synergy, who gets to know the company well.

SIXTEEN

FLOTATIONS

FLOATING, or going public, is the natural progression of a growth company which is confident of its future and is akin to an adolescent achieving maturity. For a really good company which has a high quality of earnings, it is usually preferable to selling out, unless a trade offer is made for it at a knock-out price. The flotation process does not preclude a trade sale later, indeed it puts a value on the company which can enhance serious offers.

The essentials for a good flotation are a growing and consistent revenue stream, ideally backed by a substantial order book, a committed management team prepared to welcome and shoulder the challenges of being an independent public company and strong financial representation, both within and outside the company, enabling it to cope with the demands of shareholders and the stock market. The increasing requirements of corporate governance have put added pressures on directors, which are aggravated when company performance is disappointing, so it is important to prepare carefully for the step and to make a success of it.

Generally speaking, the valuation put on a growth company will be related to its annual growth rate and to its profitability, measured traditionally by the price:earnings ratio. In the old days, companies' PE ratios were unlikely to exceed the annual growth in turnover, expressed as a percentage figure, although nowadays the valuation is more likely to be expressed as a multiple of turnover or revenues, which is the American way. PE ratios are still important but, for growth companies, are normally secondary. The advisers chosen for the flotation are key, notably the lawyers and the lead sponsoring investment bank. The former takes the management team through the documentation and responsibilities involved and the latter prepares and puts its name to the prospectus, lining up financial support, underwriting the issue and generally guiding the company through the flotation process.

The choice of the advisers, which should involve a 'beauty parade' as it is called, should be influenced by their general reputation and their understanding of the type of business concerned. In particular, it should be geared to identifying those committed to a strong after-sales service in which they are likely to support the company through any subsequent problems. You need advisers who are not fair-weather friends and who help you through your hour of need, as and when it comes. The old adage that 'success has a hundred fathers and failure is an orphan' has sadly a lot of truth in it.

Flotations on the London Exchange in the UK are generally not too onerous, since institutions take a longer-term view and obligatory reporting is still bi-annual, although the pressures are becoming more demanding. The advantages of the Alternative Investment Market (AIM) in the UK are also appealing to a young, technology company seeking a flotation since, in addition to those covered above, it has less regulatory hurdles and is substantially cheaper than a full listing. For these reasons, many overseas companies are also attracted by the idea of an AIM float.

Flotations in the US, on for instance NASDAQ, often produce bigger up-front prices for the sale of shares at flotation but are very demanding in terms of future performance, coupled with quarterly reporting which can be a substantial burden on a company and its management. Size is also a factor in successful NASDAQ flotations, since it is bad news to be too small, and the costs of such flotations are now high, in relation, for instance, to AIM.

Once a flotation has occurred, onerous conditions are imposed on a company's reporting and, in particular, on the sale or purchase of shares by its directors and staff, with any form of insider dealing being strictly prohibited. The demands of corporate governance also become more onerous and can take a disproportionate amount of time and often become commercially self-defeating, in that they make executives risk-averse and too concerned with covering their own behaviour and liability exposure. Risks have to be taken in business and many of the bureaucratic and mechanistic actions required by corporate governance do not help, in my opinion.

Once a company has successfully floated and achieved a high price for its stock, it is in a good position to raise more money for expansion purposes through a secondary offering and to make acquisitions, using high priced paper that can limit dilution of its equity. On the downside, the liability risks for the company and its directors have grown substantially in recent years and shareholders are much more prepared to initiate class actions, along US lines, if things go wrong. Having good insurance cover for the company, and accompanying directors and officers cover for its staff, is therefore essential, if good people are going to be attracted, particularly at Board level.

Companies in growth markets that go public on a wing and a prayer – and there are a number of them – are doing a disservice to their sectors, since they are awakening unreasonable expectations in the public which, in the main, does not understand the products and technologies involved. Investors are consequently very disillusioned when the performance of such companies is disappointing, or even disastrous, and are switched off from further investment, having had their fingers burnt in the offering.

The less that people understand a company's business, the more, it seems, the valuation can be hyped to appeal to their gambling instinct. For instance, in the South Sea Bubble, several hundred years ago, a large sum of money was raised by a promoter on a project which was to be kept secret from everyone, including the investors!

If a company performs well during the span of an investment, a flotation is the natural and most satisfactory choice of exit. The management have earned their continued independence and the investor has a continuing ride, if he or she wants it, in a growth company, enhanced by having a quotation. A flotation is the point at which a company moves from a dependency on private money to public funds, but it is also satisfying to a company to see a lot of its existing shareholders stay in after the float. Not only does this indicate their confidence in the company but it also provides continuity and stability to the shareholder base.

When a company goes public, a venture capital backer often

has the opportunity to realise some of its investment, say 25%, as discussed elsewhere. A key decision is whether to run with the rest or to realise it as soon as practicable and this will depend very much on the stability and momentum of the business as well as, of course, the outlook for stock markets. Where companies have predictable and exciting revenue and earnings prospects, it is normally better to stay with the investment but, where these are uncertain or volatile, it is preferable to play safe and sell early.

Seventeen

Acquisitions and Mergers

A S DISCUSSED previously, acquisitions and mergers can be a fruitful way in which a company can accelerate its organic growth, particularly after it has gone public and has high priced paper. They can also be reciprocally a way in which an exit can be achieved by selling out to a trade buyer, either for cash or shares.

Only about one in nine acquisitions are truly successful, as mentioned earlier. The reasons for this are that people are mesmerised by the advantages of a projected deal which are usually few and large, and they overlook the disadvantages which are often many and small, but which, nevertheless, can fatally impair their success.

The key to good acquisitions is for there to be genuine commercial logic and synergy in the two entities considering joining forces, particularly with regard to markets, products and technologies. Assuming that these are there, other important factors are that the respective cultures and chemistries of the two businesses and their executives should be compatible and that the price of the deal should be fair to both sides, since they are going to have to live with the result of what they have created, assuming that the deal is a friendly one.

If all these ingredients are there, the way in which the deal is consummated and followed through is important, since staff in the companies concerned are usually initially well-disposed to changes, provided that the reasons for them are properly explained and carried out quickly. Failure to do this, in a reasonable time, will result in such staff falling back on their own company's cultures and loyalties and not being prepared to transfer them to the enlarged entity.

Making acquisitions and mergers stick is also important and

requires considerable efforts and perseverance from both sides, over a span of at least eighteen months and often longer, before things settle down. It is often necessary for a company to go through a minor crisis before people are demonstrably on the same side, having faced up to and solved problems together.

All successful relationships also require reciprocity and, whilst giving and taking will inevitably be unbalanced at any point in time, over a period both sides must feel that they have benefited from the process of amalgamation, as well as being prepared to help their sister company out, when required. It is important that the deal fulfils everyone's expectations and that synergy of 2+2=5 is clearly demonstrated.

Acquisitions and mergers are a dangerous step for investors in a private company unless the transaction concerned has been very carefully thought through and researched. They will often be asked to put up more money to enable it to happen and, if things go wrong, their base investment may also be weakened or threatened. However, judiciously and sparingly applied, acquisitions can enhance a company's value since they can accelerate its progress and give it critical mass, both from an operating and an exit point of view.

Companies, on the other hand, which make a habit of acquisition and whose growth and progress depend on them are to be avoided. The reasons for this are that risks are enhanced, due to the probability of some of the deals going wrong, and the shareholder never really knows how good progress is, since the figures are obfuscated by continuing acquisition costs, non-recurring charges and goodwill adjustments.

Mergers are even more difficult to make a success of, since compromises are needed to keep both sides of the transaction happy, particularly with regard to a sharing out of management roles and responsibilities. It is also harder to effect cost savings because each side has a natural tendency to argue the case for its own staff and resources, and indeed is expected to do so by them. Usually successful mergers are a polite name given to acquisitions to make them more palatable and they can some-times involve the reverse takeover of a large company by a smaller one. If the former is public, the process can be a cheap way of the latter going public.

Takeovers are effectively hostile acquisitions or mergers and are rarely relevant to a private company, particularly where the management control it. However, for a public company, they are a danger, usually where performance is poor and the shareholders are disgruntled.

In a contested takeover, the bidding company can expect no co-operation from the management of the target business and will normally have to rely on published information. This makes the task of the bidder more difficult which is why hostile bids are relatively rare, except at the height of an M&A boom.

Eighteen

Trade Sales

A PRIVATE company may adopt a trade sale as an alternative to flotation, if its growth rate and quality of earnings is not up to the rigours of going public, and it is also wise to go this route if its management does not want to face up to the pressures of running a public company. Such an exit may also produce a higher immediate exit valuation, often with a share offer or cash alternative, but will lose out on future growth, unless the acquirer has even more potential than the company concerned.

In a perfect scenario, the synergy of the two companies joining forces would produce a better result than the two of them on their own. In such a situation, all parties and their shareholders should benefit, although in practise such situations are rare and difficult to achieve.

Even when the synergies and chemistries are right, valuation is always an emotive issue and, in general, some compromise will be required, with the selling party getting less than it had hoped and the acquirer paying more than it had planned. Sometimes it is necessary, because of a wide gulf in value expectations between the two companies, to structure an earn-out deal, where some of the consideration is related to future earnings from the acquired company. Such deals are sometimes the only way in which a wide gap can be bridged but the earn-out period should be kept short, one to two years at most, as it tends to be a divide between the two companies while it lasts and inhibits the process of integration.

Other forms of venture capital trade sale exits are where a company has gone public and all or part of the venture capital stake has been retained, which is almost 'de rigueur' in a US flotation. In these circumstances, valuation will need to be related to the stock market capitalisation, although it is usual where change of control is involved, for there to be a 25–33⅓% premium on the share price.

Cash purchases are relatively simple to organise, with the emphasis being that the acquirer should be satisfied with its projected purchase after due diligence has been carried out, which is always easier in a private company situation than a public one. It is also likely to require reasonable warranties, usually related to an escrow account, in which a proportion of the consideration of up to, say, 20% is withheld for, at least, twelve months.

Share exchange purchases are easier from a valuation stand-point, since comparative valuations usually flatter the company being acquired. However, they are harder to conduct and implement, since both sides have to investigate each other, and warranties normally therefore have to be reciprocal. Where some of the selling shareholders want cash, they can only work if a vendor placing can be effected, in concert with the deal.

In a private company setting, the only real advisers required are two sets of lawyers for the respective companies, with, some-times, independent ones for the shareholders, if their interests are different from those of their investee company. In addition, there will, of course, need to be two firms of established auditors for the companies.

In a public company setting, one or two investment banks will also need to be appointed, depending on whether one or both of the companies are public, in order to ensure that the valuation of the deal is fair and to guide the process through the regulatory hurdles involved. The fees for such deals can become very ex-pensive and need to be carefully controlled.

The trade sale exit is usually the simplest, although not neces-sarily the best one for an investor, since the choice of action is limited. In a well-negotiated exit, the selling shareholders should have a choice of cash or shares in the acquiring company, or a combination of the two.

Investors in the private company being sold would only wish to take shares in the acquirer if it had good prospects and offered reasonable liquidity, normally through a quotation on a recog-nised exchange. Any warranties or indemnities which they give should be limited to their ownership of shares and their only other exposure should be in part of the consideration being held in an escrow account, backed by warranties from their company and its management, as discussed earlier in the chapter.

An exception to this is a trade sale based on an earn-out, where part of the consideration is contingent upon the selling company hitting pre-agreed earnings targets. In this situation, the selling company must be free to run its own affairs for the earn-out period, which is not always satisfactory from the acquirer's point of view.

Nineteen

Case Studies

IN ORDER to illustrate the material contained in the previous chapters, this one outlines four case studies that I have been personally involved with, covering in turn a start-up, a second-stage financing, a third-stage financing and a turnround. They also cover, between them, a range of strategic alliance, flotation, acquisition and trade sale experiences.

1   A Start-Up

In the mid 1990s, I had the opportunity to invest in an IT start-up in Birmingham in the UK which was based on the concept of creating a new generation of software for the international banking industry. The software, apart from being advanced itself, was conceived upon the tool-kit principle of developing a number of standard components which could be assembled together to build a cost-effective solution to a particular banking situation, rather like Ford pioneered in the automobile industry.

Established software companies in the industry have little incentive to effect major upgrades of their customers' software products, since this process usually opens up such a step to competition, apart from being fairly disruptive; as it was explained graphically to me, the Almighty took seven days to create the Universe but he did not have an installed base! A new company, on the other hand, has no such constraints and can actively go after new customers, arguing the benefits of its advanced technology.

The founder of the company had previously been a successful entrepreneur, and had assembled a management team of people whom he knew well and, in several cases, had worked with before. He was also prepared to put a substantial sum of money into the new company out of his own funds.

With some of the unknowns removed and the risks therefore limited, I decided to invest in the new company alongside another well-established venture capital group. Both I and a member of this group went onto the Board of the new company.

Initially, the company made somewhat slow progress and for the best part of eighteen months was making significant losses of about £150,000 per month, albeit within its business plan. Inevitably, the situation put pressure on the founder and his team to improve the commercial results, and he went out and found an established business with legacy products in the banking services field which we subsequently acquired at a very good price. This acquisition proved to be an inspired one, since the combination of enhanced turnover, purchased cheaply, and substantial cost reductions through integration with our technology and resources, transformed our financial results and put us into solid profitability. I was able to help in the acquisition by reassuring and helping to convince the vendor that our company's management would look after his customers, which was a major concern of his.

The combined entity went public very successfully on the main London market and at a substantially increased valuation to the original investment, with all outstanding preferred capital and loans being repaid. Existing investors were able to sell 25% of their stake at the float but were required to keep the remainder for the time being.

The company asked me to stay on the Board for the float, which I did, but it was a somewhat mixed blessing, because when the technology boom arrived, prices went through the roof, and I was unable to sell when I wanted to. The other venture capitalist, who was not on the Board at the time, was able, on the other hand, to exit the rest of his stake at a very substantial valuation.

2   A Second-Stage Financing

In the late 1980s one of my company's venture capital funds was winding up and one of the US investments in the fund, based in California, had not yet reached its full potential. After getting an independent valuation, I therefore offered the fund's investors the opportunity to back a buy-out of the business concerned, which had a turnover of over $10 million, with a combination of equity, redeemable debentures and bank loan, since the balance sheet concerned was suited to a reasonably geared transaction. The redeemable debentures had an escalating yield, going from 5% to 10% over five years, and with this incentive, the debentures were repaid over the first three years of the investment, after the bank loan had been cleared. I remember the company's CFO mournfully observing when the interest rate rose to a high level on the debentures that he 'used to love those babies'.

Whilst the company, of which I was Chairman, had to be run for cash flow in its initial phase in order to enable the debt to be serviced and repaid, the real intention was to concentrate on the company's high margin products in the medical electronics field, and expand them on the international market, which was duly done. I knew the company's CEO and his team well and he, with its help, did an excellent job in repositioning the company for growth, motivated by the challenge and by the fact that they now had a 25% stake in their own company.

Revenues rose to over $20 million and profitability was well over 10%, with the company having a strong balance sheet. We considered taking the company public on NASDAQ but the appetite on that Exchange at the time was for faster growing and more speculative ventures, which we clearly were not. We, therefore, having prepared a draft prospectus, decided to accept a very good approach and offer from a European quoted company in the healthcare sector, which was acceptable and well-known to the management.

Investors, including the management, made ninety times their money in cash on their original equity, and those who took paper in the acquirer and kept it for several years, increased this to 450 times. Everyone, therefore, was well satisfied by the outcome.

3   A Third-Stage Financing

In 1990, I met a British expatriate who had set up his own business on the East Coast of America. He had, at that time, built up a company providing clinical trials services to pharmaceutical companies seeking regulatory approval for their new drugs, with a revenue base of $15 million and a net income of $1 million.

I got on well with the company's founder and liked his concept of building up a group capable of offering a full service, through Phases I–IV of clinical trials, to the pharmaceutical majors on an international basis. He was very much pre-occupied with internationalising the business, which is why he chose me to go on the Board and my firm to make a major and lead investment in his company, through our managed funds.

The founder and most of his management team were very bright scientists with limited formal business training. He, however, had a natural commercial flair and my job was to help him and his team learn and apply formal methods, such as the introduction of proper monthly budgets and management accounts, which are essential to have in place in order to be able to service and control growth. It was an enjoyable task because bright people learn quickly and make things work.

The company went public, three years after our investment, on NASDAQ and consistently produced excellent quarterly results for the next four years that I was on the Board. As its rating rose, it carried out a number of fruitful secondary public offerings, and used its now high priced paper to make a number of tactical acquisitions within its focused strategy of becoming a full-service international services group.

The investment was a highly successful one for us, which was just as well, as it was the biggest that I have ever made. I was on the Board for nearly seven years and, in that time, the company's revenues and profits grew very substantially – the former to over $1 billion – and the share price rose from $1.50 to over $50 per share. My involvement was an exhilarating, although demanding one and, apart from being on the Holdings Board, I was on the Executive Committee and was Chairman of the Audit Committee.

4   A Turnround

In the early 1980s, I was Chairman of a technology fund whose aim was to encourage the transfer of technology between Britain and North America, by investing in companies active in that sphere. In that capacity, I was approached by a government sponsored body and a leading private equity firm to buy their combined stake in a UK public company, which was just over 30%. As they accurately put it, the company, which had many current problems, needed new management and money.

The company was an established name, and had a long history in scientific and industrial instruments, serving the military aviation market and, to a lesser extent, the commercial market. It was, when I first saw it, making a loss of £1.5 million with borrowings of over $4 million, which was a lot of money in those days.

After much thought and careful scrutiny, I decided to make a bid for the company, which had a full listing on the London Exchange, aided by a leading merchant bank and stockbroker. After two extensions of what the *Evening Standard* called 'a cheeky bid', we were able to obtain more than the necessary 90% acceptance from existing shareholders required to take the company private and compulsorily buy-out the minorities.

On day one of the bid, I became Chairman and changed the shareholders, top management and existing bank, and concentrated on reorientating the business and bringing through the management in the layer below, who knew the business well and were therefore critical to its future. The immediate task was to cut out unprofitable products, reduce costs and overheads, and sell off unprofitable businesses, for what we could get for them.

One of the biggest headaches was that the company had a large unoccupied property site with very high rental costs on a long lease. I went to see the property business that owned the site, before finalising the takeover and managing to negotiate a favourable deal to exit the premises within one year. However, my self-congratulations were premature as, following the takeover, I found that the company had informally granted the local football club the right to use part of the land as a pitch many years before, although no records of an agreement were available. After protracted negotiations, a solution was found and the site was handed over, with vacant possession.

I remember at the outset, after completing the bid, when stress was at a high point, the company's house journal coming out with the heading 'A warm welcome from your new chairman' and a picture of me with a balloon from my mouth and the caption 'You're fired!' The effect was compounded by the fact that my attempt to smile in a nerve-wracking situation looked more like a sinister sneer.

After the initial actions had been taken, progress was made reasonably quickly and the company turned round after its first year. This process was aided by a good tactical acquisition which expanded the profitable part of the business: aviation instruments.

It was unwise, however, to breathe a sigh of relief and relax because this profitable part, which I had not touched, then ran into difficulties and it was necessary to cut costs there as well. I always felt that it was a bit like being told to go back into the ring with a leading heavyweight, after surviving the initial bout.

Fortunately, the secondary surgery worked, and the group moved into respectable profitability, albeit after a rights issue. We started to consider re-floating the company but had a series of escalating bids from an established quoted UK group in the sector, the last of which we eventually accepted, turning a total investment of £7.5 million into a sale consideration of £16.5 million in less than five years. The IRR was 28.37% and I particularly enjoyed indirectly selling back, at a handsome profit, our stake to the private equity firm that we had first bought the company from, who were investors in the acquiring group.

I learnt, during this turnround, which was in my early days in venture capital, that there are easier ways of earning a living. In particular, it is sensible to put scarce management and finance into growth situations where the upside is unlimited, instead of turnrounds where the reverse is true and the efforts and stresses are as great, if not greater.

In the four cases studies dealt with above, it will be noted that two of the companies were in healthcare and two in technology and that two of them were British and two North American. One of the UK ones floated on the London Exchange with a full listing and one of the US ones floated on NASDAQ, with the other two exiting through trade sales to quoted companies. Several of the companies were active in the strategic alliance and acquisition fields during my involvement with them.

Twenty

International Niche Businesses

M UCH OF THE material leading up to this Chapter has been concerned with the creation and development of international growth businesses in sectors such as healthcare and technology, and the case studies in the previous Chapter give some examples of companies that I have been involved with in this area. Usually the key to success for a young growth company is to have a narrow product focus and to exploit this as widely as practicable in the international market. As touched on earlier in the book, such companies are often called international niche businesses, the best of which concentrate on what they know and do it extremely well. In any theatre of life, a person is more likely to be successful sticking to what he or she is trained for and has become proficient in, rather than branching out into new spheres of activity which are foreign. It is possible, and sometimes necessary, for a business to broaden out and diversify, once it is established, but the process takes time, money and patience and, even then, there are risks attached. A sporting parallel would be a tennis professional taking up golf: the transition is not impossible, and indeed there are a number of examples where it has been successfully achieved, but he or she would be wise to keep the day job during the learning process!

The whole purpose of creating and developing an international niche business is to concentrate on reaping the rewards of its strengths and, at the same time, to minimise the risks in order to give a high reward/low risk profile which is what we all seek, but rarely find in an imperfect world. The high reward is optimised by exploiting the company's products and technology in a wide international market and the low risk is achieved by avoiding dangerous distractions and by keeping the central costs and overheads of the business as low as possible. This enables it to maintain its entrepreneurial flair and flavour and to be quick on its feet, when faced with both opportunities and threats. This is particularly true in a fast-changing world where speed and flexibility are vital, if the fate of the dinosaur is to be avoided!

The thinking behind an international niche business is based upon the rifleshot approach, rather than the scattergun one in which money and resources are thrown at a problem in the hope that two or three pellets will strike home. I remember in my youth watching a rifle-shooting competition in which a marksman with a single-shot weapon scored 31 bulls-eyes out of 35 shots, compared to one with an automatic weapon who obtained 30 bulls-eyes with 350 shots, in the same period of time. Unless a venture capitalist has very large financial resources, and a large slice of luck, he or she is better off adopting the rifle-shot approach in which every shot tells, particularly in countries where investors have limited financial resources and do not like major risks being taken with their money.

The traditional wisdom conversely in venture capital is that the portfolio approach, based on the scattergun principle, is the norm and that, in a fund, two or three major winners will make a success of the portfolio, particularly where large amounts of money are being managed. Whilst it is true that several major winners will raise the profile of the fund, I do not see this as incompatible with making every shot tell, since failure is to be avoided, if at all possible. Such an approach, which is the one that I have sought to adopt, is only possible if a manageable amount of money is being put to work and adequate attention is being paid to all of the investments in the fund. As discussed later, I believe that there will be great demand in the future for venture capital companies which combine the management of limited funds with the provision of constructive and professional services to young growth companies, effectively combining relatively small amounts of finance with lots of help.

The international niche business is particularly relevant for a company in a country with a small domestic market, such as most of those within the European Union. It is vital for such companies to seek and achieve exports early in their life, if they are to grow organically. This is in marked contrast to the past priorities of companies in countries with larger domestic markets where a solid business has been able to be built in the home field before striking out internationally. Having said that, the time-scale of change is now so fast and potential competition so great, that these companies are striking out earlier into overseas markets, even where they have large domestic markets of their own. The perfect combination is, of course, to be successful on both home and overseas fronts which is possible in countries such as the USA and Japan, but more difficult in Europe, until such time as the Single Market there becomes a reality.

Many international businesses will have strategic regional centres from which they can tackle the global market and the classic ones have to date been Europe, North America and Japan, in sectors such as the pharmaceutical one. The world is, however, becoming a wider-spread and more challenging place with fast growing economies in countries such as China, India and Russia, and the traditional centres will need to be added to or changed, with a consequent increase in complexity for international niche businesses. To cope with this, it is vital that the right balance should be struck behind those functions which are centrally carried out for the business and those that are delegated to local areas, albeit with some regional control. I remember listening many years ago to a Reith Lecture in London given by Lester Pearson, the Prime Minister of Canada at the time, in which he said that the world would be a better place if it was able to co-ordinate centrally those activities such as economic policy, trade co-operation and defence which are in everyone's interests, and decentralise locally those matters such as culture, education and administration which are best left to local communities. Sadly, these priorities are often reversed in major Government and Inter-Government Organisations, with their tendency towards bureaucracy, and this must not be allowed to happen in inter-national niche businesses. With the latter, there should be clear central co-ordination of key strategic and policy issues and good delegation of local operations, coupled to effective financial monitoring of results.

In the past, many international businesses have been built on strong brand names which allowed their products to be sold on a global basis. This applied particularly to the consumer markets in the years after the Second World War and most major companies in that era had strong brand names for themselves and their products. Brand names are still important but, with new avenues of communication, marketing and purchasing, made possible by e-mail and the Internet, a company's products and technology are equally, if not more important, since consumers can more easily pick and choose what they buy. For this reason, having a strong and protected IPR is vital for a growth company.

This pattern of having excellent products and technology, with good protection, is likely to have even greater emphasis in the future as the world becomes more and more competitive and as centres of technical excellence spread. Cost will clearly also continue to be of great importance as consumers and purchasers are able to evaluate the quality and prices of competitive products in an increasingly sophisticated way, using electronic technology.

The constraints to international niche businesses will hopefully reduce with a new generation of management which has a positive inclination to international trading and is free of, and impatient with, the national biases and constraints which previous generations have experienced and been influenced by. Such businesses should be able to ply their trade sensitively and in co-operation with local interests and priorities and without too much concentration of power, which can generate local antagonism. This is very important in a world in which there is beginning to be a reaction against the excesses of globalisation and there is a movement towards trade protectionism in some quarters, in order to preserve local jobs and customs. Where a company moves from being an international niche business to become a fully-fledged and broader-based business in its own right, it has normally moved on from venture capital backing, since the latter has a finite time-span of up to seven years or so. If its diversification is carried out sensibly, then its enlarged base will give it breadth and stability as it continues to grow and develop. Where diversification plans go wrong, usually because companies have become top-heavy and too widely spread, it often makes sense for the business to be privatised and reduced back to its core activity, effectively being restored to international niche status.

The next two Chapters set out respectively the main results and findings of the development and financing experiences which I have had with international niche businesses over a thirty-five year span. Whilst my direct venture capital involvement has been mainly with European and North American companies, split more or less equally, I have also had a good deal of involvement with other parts of the world, as chairman or director of a number of international companies over the years, coupled to earlier international consultancy assignments. In putting forward these results and findings, it is necessary to qualify them because of the continuing speed of change which, if anything is accelerating, and future opportunities and challenges are likely to be very different in some respects from those of the past. Adaptability is, therefore, essential.

Twenty-One

International Development

AN INTERNATIONAL niche business has been defined earlier as a business with wide market scope and a narrow product focus which enables it to retain its flexibility as it grows and, at the same time, keep its production costs and overheads low. The way in which such a business can be developed is now examined under the headings of market scope, product focus, staff management and cost control.

1   Market Scope

Whether a potential international niche business is based in Europe, North America, Japan or elsewhere, the challenge is the same of coupling the creation of a profitable domestic business with the development of a strong overseas one, as early as practicable. In developed overseas markets, the choice of marketing method can involve an agent, an exclusive distributor, setting up a joint venture, having one's own company or making an acquisition. With a new technology-based product, it is often advisable to set up one's own company initially and then move on to make an acquisition in support of it, if sufficient progress is made and added resources are required. Agents and distributors are a cheaper entry point but may not be able to bring sufficient understanding and attention to the sales of the new products involved.

In Asia and the developing world, it is normally necessary to have a local partner with the required contacts and credibility with customers, who are often government related, and major contracts are difficult to get without such a partner's help and involvement. The selection of the right partner is an important and difficult task which, to be successful, must involve mutual trust and a similar attitude to money, amongst other things.

Different countries have different approaches to business. For instance in North America, there is a major emphasis on strategy and business is played like a national sport, with a strong emphasis on team building and an even stronger one on being competitive and winning. There are no prizes for coming second!

In Japan, there is great emphasis on establishing relationships over, say, at least a couple of years, before entering into business with someone new. It is also a very polite society where people appear to agree with you, when actually they do not wish to be rude by disagreeing publicly. This can be misleading, and it should be remembered that silence does not necessarily mean consent.

Every country has its pluses and minuses and I remember a long time ago being advised by a very successful Chinese businessman that an outsider can often see an opportunity in a foreign country more clearly than its indigenous population. He certainly proved that point and, over the years, I have come to benefit from that approach myself, in selective instances.

The philosophy of looking in from the outside can often be taken further by backing an expatriate from one's own country when seeking to exploit opportunities within a large country such as the United States. It also has the added advantage of a common approach to strategy and the management of money, often on a more frugal basis than would otherwise be available. I have had very happy experiences in adopting this concept on a number of occasions.

I have had a range of involvements in international niche businesses starting with doing some work for a leading 4x4 vehicle company in the 1960's, which has been a classically successful example over many years. Another involvement was as Chairman of a Savile Row tailor in the 1970's which started taking its wares to the international market. Its Managing Director, when asked by a somewhat aggressive overseas customer 'How many of your suits are good?', gave the immortal reply 'About 1 in 10, the rest are excellent!' In the last twenty years, most of my involvements have been as chairman or director of a number of international healthcare and technology companies which all had a wide market spread and relatively narrow product focus, with a majority of them having a regional spread covering Europe, North America, Japan and the Far East.

2   Product Focus

The importance of IPR, and its protection, has been emphasised elsewhere in this book, although the obtaining of patents is often easier than their enforcement for a small company. This trend will gather momentum, as more and more countries and businesses enter the competitive fray and as development expenditures increase in countries, such as Japan which takes a long-term view, and in China and India which wish to move up from low-cost jobs and economic activity.

It is vital that successful international niche businesses keep control of their IPR and maintain their technical lead in their chosen fields of endeavour. To exploit their potential, they will, however, wish to make judicious use of licensing, both on an exclusive and non-exclusive basis, as appropriate.

3   Staff Management

The first time that I talked to a potential overseas employee for a British company, a manager quizzed me on my return home to ask whether I had really stressed the international benefits of the job, and I replied that I had because I outlined the company's worldwide potential. I remember him answering 'Are you sure you stressed the real benefits of, for instance, trips to London?'! The use of such side benefits and motivations in international business, whilst not to be ignored, has to be kept under close control and within strictly legal limits. As a Middle-East client said to me at about that time, 'You British are too straight-laced but that is why we do business with you!'

I remember the first time which I met the owner of a business in Southern Europe that I, as a company chairman, was thinking of acquiring, he said 'I have brought you a present'. Somewhat wrong-footed, I turned round and took off my tie, which fortunately was a new one, and was able to reciprocate. The point of this story is that it is important to understand local customs and respond to them, if a positive dialogue and mutual understanding is to be established.

I have always enjoyed working in the United States, because of the emphasis on sport and the strong competitive spirit that exists there. Having started as a tennis player, it was a natural extension of business to take up golf and I have many happy memories, plus some moments to forget, of playing on some great courses, including Augusta National, with the management and staff of the companies that I have been involved with.

Another demanding but enjoyable requirement in the US is the need for management to give time to meet all the staff regularly, both by going round the premises and collectively. I remember the first time that I stood up on a soap-box as chairman of a US company and addressed a multi-racial audience, I heard the sardonic comments of three executives behind me. These were in sequence 'Only half laughed at his jokes', 'Only half understood him' and 'It was not the same half!' Despite this faltering start, I have had very positive experiences working with US companies, not only on golf courses but also in the financial results which have been achieved, as well as considerable enjoyment and satisfaction over many years.

It is important to pick good people in any country but it is more difficult to find and select them in overseas territories. The qualities of excellence, trust and reciprocation to be looked for are the same but are sometimes cloaked by local customs, languages and pre-conceived notions. With the right person it is possible to have a close rapport even though separated by 5,000 miles, whilst with the wrong one it does not matter how close or far apart you both are, although the problem is easier to resolve when it is near at hand.

Finally, I have learnt in working with successful entrepreneurs that they are often prepared to relocate for a period of, say, two years to establish their business in an overseas region in their own mould, before putting permanent management in place. They are effectively the lightning rod necessary to make the initial breakthrough, which is a different skill to the on-going management of the business.

4   Cost Control

Every business must have a good financial control system and an international niche one is no exception, in fact it is even more necessary with it often having a plethora of overseas countries and nationalities.

The business must, however, be structured to serve its customers and its commercial units, with overheads being kept to a necessary minimum. In this, the concept of zero budgeting, which challenges the validity of any spend, needs to be applied with overheads only included if they are essential.

Direct costs also need to be kept to a minimum, with manufacture often being sub-contracted out to a low-cost area or country. It is usual, however, to keep control of final assembly and, in the US when a breakthrough is made, it is often necessary to back up early success with local manufacturing resources to meet escalating demand, which can otherwise be overpowering in such a large market.

TWENTY-TWO

INTERNATIONAL FINANCING

THE FINANCING of international niche businesses is explored below under the headings of corporate structure, local partners, professional advisers and venture capital support.

1   Corporate Structure

As a company grows through its various evolutionary stages to become an international niche business, its corporate structure will need to develop to cope with both central and local needs in the overseas countries in which it has a presence. In this process, the structure of the overall company should be kept as simple as possible, consistent with local legal requirements and tax issues, which are often complicated. It is usually beneficial to obtain local representation on the Board of any overseas companies so that a watching brief can be maintained. This, although helpful, is no substitute for regular contact with and visits from central management, coupled to an effective financial control system.

To date, the main venture capital operating and investment areas have been the US, the UK and Continental Europe, all of which have established industrial infrastructures and stock markets, as well as well-defined legal systems and codes of ethics. This situation is changing rapidly and venture capital firms are increasingly extending their operations into other less well-defined and regulated territories, which will both provide great opportunities and great risks. Hopefully, these risks will reduce as local infrastructures and laws are built up in the future.

2   Local Partners

My first experience in the US was to co-invest with a leading firm who brought me in on the deal, albeit for a small amount. When things went wrong which they did, it decided to write the investment off and I was powerless to do anything else. That is when I learnt the real meaning of the phrase 'caveat emptor'!

On the back of this and similar passive involvements, I decided that my firm would replicate its pro-active approach in the US, since pulling out of investing there was the only alternative. I duly, therefore, bought a house in San Francisco in 1980 and spent a lot of time developing the firm's US business which served it very well over the years.

The lesson that I learnt is that you have to play the game which you know, if you are to succeed and, since that time, we have had a number of very successful US investments. Some of these have involved local venture capital partners who are happy for us to play a pro-active role alongside them, particularly with regard to the internationalisation of a business which has been our particular interest and experience.

Once a reputation for international help has been established, there is a complementary fit with local venture capital firms which welcome working with someone who can add that value. In one instance, I was brought in to an investment in the US by a venture capital firm there because the CEO was British and wanted a kindred spirit on the Board to help with its international challenges, prior to flotation.

3   Professional Advisers

Having good professional advisers when dealing with overseas companies and investors is a 'sine qua non' as far as I am concerned. Only then can the particular accounting and legal problems be properly understood and dealt with. Other areas of importance are tax and associated matters such as inter-company pricing, which can have ramifications for the company, both locally and centrally.

It is also important to have good relationships with local banks who are more likely to be sympathetic to local businesses. Apart from helping the development of these businesses, they are vital to have in place if the investment in the local subsidiary is realised through, for instance, a flotation on a local exchange or through a trade sale.

Handling the impact of different currencies is sometimes a difficult task with an international business, and getting good foreign exchange advice from a commercial or investment bank can help a great deal in limiting the company's exposure and setting up hedging contracts. Another important principle is to match overseas currency assets and liabilities as far as possible, and it is usually good practice for any overseas borrowings by subsidiaries to be restricted to their local currency.

When it comes to deals or realisations, I prefer to do them myself with good legal and accounting help rather than through brokers or investment banks. It is certainly cheaper and facilitates direct contact with the other party's management; this approach is, of course, more difficult where the other party is a public company.

4 Venture Capital Support

Details of the venture capital support for international niche business covers Board involvements (both centrally and locally, where appropriate), overseas introductions, help on strategy and some operational matters, acquisitions and realisations and, of course, money. The main contribution is the ability to assist in the myriad of tasks required for the company to evolve into a successful international niche business over a number of years, based on the venture capitalist's previous comprehensive experience. Further details of these tasks are described later in the book.

TWENTY-THREE

FUND STRUCTURES AND MANAGEMENT

W HEN modern venture capital started in the UK in the 1970s, the only fund structures available there were ones involving a loose association of pension funds and other tax-exempt institutions on the one hand, and a private limited company for non-exempt taxpayers and institutions on the other. The first of these worked well, although the money was generally all put in up-front and only paid out at the end, to the detriment of investor liquidity and return. The second was tax-inefficient, since built-up gains were subject to double capital gains tax, the only escape from which was to go public and become an authorised investment trust.

In the 1980s, distributing vehicles became available in the form of authorised unit trusts (which could be public if required by investors), and limited partnerships, which provided transparency for individuals on tax, with early losses being available for offset against personal gains elsewhere. These more modern vehicles were based on the principle of calling down money as needed over, say, a three year initial period and then distributing back realisations to investors, as they were made in the second half of the life of the fund, normally years five to ten. Such distributing vehicles can either be UK-based or located in low-tax areas, such as Jersey or Bermuda.

UK vehicles can be directly managed by venture capital managers, but off-shore ones need to have a local manager, usually an overseas subsidiary of the UK venture firm, with the latter being an investment adviser to the fund. US funds, on the other hand, are normally US based and, of these, the

Delaware limited partnership, managed by a local General Partner, is the most common.

As explored later in Chapter Twenty-Eight, returns of 16% or so per annum can be expected from a good venture capital fund. Whilst this is not as high as recent returns in the UK buy-out field, they should be more consistent over the longer term, because they are less dependent on interest rates and economic conditions, under which leveraging can become a disadvantage, as was evidenced in the early 1970s and 1990s. In the US, there is more volatility of return, with very high figures being achieved at the height of the dot-com boom in the second half of the 1990s matched by some substantial losses in the early 2000s with the rumoured 90 and 99 Clubs available for those who lost that percentage share of their investments in the latter period!

There should be more emphasis on the long-term performance of venture capital firms rather than a preoccupation with the last fund, if volatile swings of support are to be avoided. Sound firms, with sensible teams and policies, learn from their mistakes and warrant long-term backing, if the real venture capital industry is to become a meaningful entity in this country.

Turning to the management of a venture capital fund and firm, it is important that, firstly, the fund should have a clear policy in an area in which the firm and its staff have experience. It is also important that the fund's investments stay within this policy, as otherwise the money has been raised for it on a false premise and prospectus.

Secondly, there should be proper routines for identifying, evaluating, approving, completing, monitoring and realising investments, so that a disciplined process is applied to the management of the money. Thirdly, there should be a clear plan to build up a balanced portfolio of investments to spread risk, both in terms of stage of investment and geographical deployment. Start-up funds that concentrate on early-stage investments only, as in the transfer of university technology, are notoriously difficult to achieve commercial returns on, as the investments all have the same risk profiles, with problems becoming apparent early and rewards from portfolio companies often taking a long time to come through.

The management of the venture capital firm itself is not technically difficult as, from a financial standpoint, there will be a few large and predictable streams of fee income from its managed funds, coupled with a limited number of costs, of which the main two are staff and property. From the point of view of building and managing a balanced team, however, it is more of a challenge as a lot of people in the investment world are prima donnas, preoccupied with their own roles and rewards. The job of being a chairman or managing partner of a venture capital firm is, therefore, somewhat similar to that of the conductor of an orchestra who seeks to ensure that everyone plays his own instrument in harmony to the benefit of the whole.

Finally, it is vital that a firm's strategy should be carefully thought out, and expressed in, amongst other things, a well-defined investment policy. A focused strategy is a vital weapon in obtaining good deals and performing thereafter in a highly competitive world in which you have to know what you are doing, and do it very well.

Twenty-Four

Investment Processes

A ssuming that a venture capital firm has a clear and focused strategy and a good and balanced team of staff to implement it, the firm's third requirement will be to have disciplined investment processes covering the identification, evaluation and approval, completion, monitoring and realisation of investments. The bigger the firm, and the more money that it manages, the greater the importance of formalising these processes, which are now explored in chronological sequence.

1   Identifying Investments

There is always a lot of talk in the venture capital industry about deal flow but, in my experience, the good opportunities very rarely come through the door or the mail. Those that do have done the rounds and are either too expensive or nobody wants them.

Whilst a venture capitalist has to look at cold opportunities that turn up out of the blue, and respond to them professionally and politely, the chance of success is equivalent to looking for a pearl in a bed of oysters. The important thing is to make up one's mind quickly about each deal so as not to waste too much time on it or the time of the person presenting it.

Where a deal is introduced by a contact, it is equally important to evaluate the quality that can be expected from the person concerned. Sadly, many people, and often the most persistent ones, have a habit of turning up repeatedly with poor deals and once again, it is necessary to respond to the approach diplomatically but without wasting too much time.

Conversely, there are a few contacts who can be expected to

come up with good quality deals and they naturally get one's full attention. Generally, such people have thought carefully about the opportunity and have sought to introduce it to a counterpart who they feel can be of help to it, as an honest broker should.

Good contacts, if one can term them that, can be friends, financial sources who have a wide network, or industry executives, who have had previous experience of the venture capital firm in question, and are able to recommend it to their clients and colleagues. Word of mouth is, therefore, very important in the industry, as is the reputation of the venture capitalist concerned, both in terms of integrity and fair dealing and in his or her capability to contribute and add value to the opportunity concerned.

In order to stimulate a flow of such opportunities, it is necessary to make people aware of the venture capital firm's strategy and areas of competence and, in particular, to let them know and be very clear about the type of companies that are being sought by the firm. This, coupled with a genuinely good reputation for work, is the key to finding good opportunities.

Sometimes it is necessary to be even more proactive, and to put a proposition to a company or person where a new opportunity is identified in the market. In such a situation, the venture capitalist is acting as a technological impresario in setting in train, and helping to finance, a new development which might not otherwise occur. In such instances, the firm is effectively creating its own deal.

2   Evaluating and Approving Investments

The first stage in evaluating an investment is to get some preliminary information on the company being investigated and then to meet its owner and key management. In this and subsequent meetings, it is necessary to have a delicate balancing act. The venture capitalist needs to form a clear judgement on the attractions of the opportunity through searching interrogation but, at the same time, to convey an impression to the company's executives that he or she is the person that they are looking for. There is no point in conducting a detailed appraisal and telling the management that they have passed muster, only to find that you have not.

Assuming, on the other hand, that the dialogue progresses favourably, the venture capitalist will need to prepare a short, ideally three page, preliminary investment memorandum covering:

- a description of the business and of its history
- an outline of its strategy, with particular reference to its market and product policy
- CVs on its key management and other important personnel
- an explanation of its resources and future requirements
- its financial record to date and future projections, often set out on a spreadsheet
- details of the investment required and the sort of IRR that can be expected, given some assumptions on entry and exit valuation.

The object of this exercise is to test, through the document, that the opportunity meets the venture capital firm's criteria in principle and that the valuation being asked for is credible. The document has the added advantage that it provides a forum for a firm's partners to discuss the project at an early stage and to decide whether to proceed further, before too much time is lost or too much money is expended on the proposition.

If the venture capital partners agree to proceed, and the company's management has a similar view, then detailed due diligence should be mounted on the investment prospect. As discussed earlier, this should entail:

- a review of the company's annual audited accounts, ideally for three to five years
- a review of its management accounts and budget for the current year
- a study of important legal documents, such as contracts, leases and patents
- investigation of the management team by talking to references and key people who know it

- visits to the company's main sites
- a detailed study of the company's products and technologies, ideally including a live demonstration in a working environment
- a review of the company's main markets, through a combination of desk research and key interviews with approved customers and industry specialists.

The results of this investigation, carried out largely by the venture capital team, would be used to prepare a final investment memorandum which would be submitted to the firm's partners for a final decision. If the firm's funds have outside directors or investment advisory groups, they would also be consulted and would need to give their approval to an investment, within the routines established in the firm. These often have to be carried out in a defined sequence and manner to meet tax requirements, particularly for overseas funds.

Formats for the preliminary and final investment memoranda are included in Appendix IV. These provide a framework for the investigations required but need to be applied intelligently and varied to suit particular deals.

3   Completing Investments

Once the necessary approvals have been obtained, proper documents for the transaction will need to be prepared by the investee company's lawyers. These will comprise contracts of purchase and sale, shareholder agreements, employment contracts and other associated documents relating to the deal. The venture capital investor or investors will need to employ their own lawyer to represent their interests, where these diverge from those of the company.

The issues that normally cause the most trouble and steam on a deal relate to financial and legal matters. The main financial ones cover the proceeds to be paid and escrow money to be held back, and the main legal ones cover the warranties and indemnities being given, primarily by the company and its management.

Assuming that the deal moves to a satisfactory completion,

and often there are at least half a dozen occasions when this seems threatened, then both sides have earned a brief celebration, before getting down to the business of working together to make the company and the investment a success. Often the gestation period for a deal from start to finish can be quite long, up to nine months, but a long engagement has the advantage of both sides getting to know each other well and to learn what to expect down the road ahead. At least, such an outcome avoids the charge of 'marry in haste and repent at leisure'.

4   Monitoring Investments

The word 'monitoring' is an expression of the venture capital firm's professional and fiduciary responsibility to its backers to 'keep tabs' on the investments that it has made on their behalf. Such monitoring is an essential task for the firm and involves the frequent review of a company's financial performance through its audited and management accounts. Most firms, therefore, have fact sheets for each of their investments which are regularly updated and reviewed, both for the firm and the fund Boards that it advises or manages.

Monitoring an investment is, however, a passive role and a good venture capitalist, appointed to the investee company's Board at the time of the investment, will wish to play an active role with the company in order to help its development and meet the added value expectations of its personnel.

The involvement of a venture capitalist on the Board can be for a period of, say, five to ten years and, in that time, he should:

- keep a firm eye, as a Board member, on the company's financial and general performance
- contribute to the normal Board agenda and discussions
- assist in the review of the executive team and play a part in key appointments
- act on the Board's sub-committees, with particular reference to the audit and remuneration committees
- advise on major developments, such as acquisitions or the opening up of new overseas offices and markets

- advise on realisation options, from flotations to trade sales
- carry out ad hoc work commissioned by the Board, where his experience has particular relevance.

Some of the activities listed may require the investee company to raise new money and the venture capital Board member will obviously be able to contribute to this. It will often be desirable for his firm to put up a lead stake for a new private round, since new investors usually like to see the existing ones come in to a round to give, amongst other things, credibility to its price. The existence of a positive relationship between the investee company and the venture capitalist is, therefore, a major asset in this process.

5   Realising Investments

The exits for a venture capital investment will normally be at a flotation or trade sale. The flotation route, however, is unlikely to offer a complete realisation since existing shareholders are usually limited in the shares that they can sell at the offering. On the London Markets, 25% is usually the maximum, whilst on NASDAQ a complete lock-in is often required for a six-month period. This can work to the venture capital firm's advantage in good flotations, since the stock often climbs dramatically after a float, if the company concerned continues to perform.

With either a float or a trade sale, the venture capital director has a major role to play in order to make sure that a good deal is done for the company and that the right documentation and terms are put in place. He will also be able to help in the choice of lawyers and investment bankers, where appropriate.

Once a venture capital investment has been realised, often in stages over a period of time, a calculation will be made of the IRR returned from the proceeds, which will be returned (through the venture capital funds involved) to the investors. At that point, the venture capital director will normally come off the Board. He or she will then look for the next opportunity with, hopefully, another good reference in the bag!

Twenty-Five

Investment Examples

T HIS CHAPTER sets out four investment examples which
illustrate the way in which the investment processes,
described in the previous one, are used. The four examples
are an early-stage Internet solutions company, a second-stage
medical communications company and two later-stage industrial instrumentation and pharmaceutical services companies,
with all of which I had Board involvement. The main text is
supported by Appendix V which contains the relevant
Investment Memoranda for the four investment propositions,
two of which are in healthcare and two in technology.

1 An Early-Stage Internet Solutions Company

In 1999, I was introduced to an Internet solutions company in
London which was looking for venture capital to fund its expansion and acquisition plans. The situation was a competitive
one, which we ended up winning, and duly put £2.5 million into
the company linked to a Board seat.

We knew the sector, but not the company, well and therefore
had to do a lot of due diligence on the latter. We also had to look
carefully at the small acquisition which it had in its sights, consequent to the venture capital financing being put in place.

The aim was to prepare the company for a flotation on the full
London Market which duly took place during the ensuing year.
We relinquished our Board place at that time and sold 25% of our
stock, which was the maximum permitted for existing shareholders.

The investment was an untypical one as far as I was concerned,
since our management involvement was short-lived and we

were tempted to sell early because of the high exit valuations available at that time. Whilst it was, therefore, more opportunistic than usual, we still achieved a good return.

2   A Second-Stage Medical Communications Company

At an early stage of my venture capital career I had a happy experience as a director of a medical publishing company which was, in due course, sold at a very attractive price. I got to know its Managing Director well and, in discussion with him after he had fulfilled his contractual obligations to the purchaser, the idea emerged of forming a new medical communications company which would develop a range of controlled-circulation medical journals in the UK and the US, backed by pharmaceutical advertising. The theme of the new company would be to provide serious medical educational material to general practitioners, hospital doctors and other medical staff.

As I knew the market and the founder well, the risks were reduced and were largely down to how long it would take to build a revenue stream from the pharmaceutical companies. Since we already had in our portfolio a small medical publishing business centred on Continental Europe, I decided to put this into the new company with a view to that business, which had revenues, helping with the launch of the new activity. About £500,000 was put into the new company to start it, and some gearing was introduced in order to help the founder get a sizeable stake at a reasonable price. This gearing was only possible because the new company had an established business base, albeit a small one.

The plan was, therefore, to build up the new activity on the back of the old business and then sell the latter from strength, since it had limited growth potential and prospects. This plan was effectively carried out, albeit over a longer time-scale than originally envisaged.

Once the initial priorities had been met, the company decided to seek second-stage expansion finance with particular reference to purchasing and exploiting a new medical communications product. This was duly done.

3   An Industrial Instrumentation Company

In my consultancy days I had got to know an industrial instrumentation company based in the West Country very well and
liked many things about it. The company supplied electrical
and electronic components to a range of blue chip clients and was
solidly profitable.

When its owner approached me with the idea of making a
venture capital investment and helping the company develop
and diversify, it was clearly of interest, as again I knew the
company and its executives well. We, therefore, after careful
scrutiny of the figures, made an investment at a sensible price
and put a director on the Board.

The company ended up being a very fruitful investment for us,
as a diversification into fibre-optic components proved to be a
success, and that business was sold later at a very high price.
Once more, we used the bread and butter base of established
products and cash flow to build a higher growth business, as
originally planned, although the process took longer than
anticipated.

At the time at which the fibre-optic components business was
sold, it was necessary to spin out the residual other components
through a management buy-out which we financed. This business has subsequently prospered.

4   A Pharmaceutical Services Company

Over the years, I have had a good deal of experience of the
pharmaceutical industry, largely through investments in
the international pharmaceutical services sector. The attractions
of this sector are that companies within it have the benefit of
providing services to a range of profitable and well established
blue chip companies with whom they have relationships. Such
relationships tend to result in long-term contracts which provide
the services companies with regular and repeat business,
coupled with a long backlog of orders.

Through previous involvement in the pharmaceutical
industry, I was introduced to a UK pharmaceutical services

company which provided marketing services to pharmaceutical majors in the launch of new drugs. The company had a solid business in the UK and a burgeoning one in the US.

I did not previously know the company, although I knew the market. After extensive due diligence from our team, I became convinced that we should pursue an investment because of its growth prospects, its management and its solid financial record.

The situation was a competitive one which we won in the end, although we had to pay rather more for our investment than I would have ideally wished. We duly made an investment linked to having a place on the Board, with the aim of helping to grow the business internationally. The plans worked out and the business developed, although the exit was a trade sale to a US buyer rather than a flotation, which was my original expectation.

As discussed, the four examples illustrate the advantages of knowing the markets and the key people involved, since this knowledge reduces the variables which, in turn, reduce the risks in an investment. However, such knowledge must be coupled with proper due diligence, conducted and set out in disciplined form, before making an investment. Even then, a successful outcome to an investment often takes longer than anticipated, although good financial track records in investee companies normally produce happy endings!

Twenty-Six

Future Developments

T HE ECONOMIC and commercial framework, within which venture capital is operating, has changed substantially over the last thirty years and will continue to change in the future, with the pace of change probably accelerating. These changes are now explored under the headings of markets, products, internationalisation and people, and with the general premise that they will, on balance, substantially enhance the attractions of venture capital as an investment sector in the years ahead.

1 Markets

In the past most venture capital investments have been made in developed economies such as the US, UK and Continental Europe, since these regions have had an established framework of business practice, laws and financial systems and markets. They have also been the dominating regions in economic terms, until recently.

With the widening of markets in emerging countries, and the rise of new industrial powers such as China and India, there is a far wider spread of opportunities for venture capital backed companies which will essentially have to treat 'the world as their oyster'. In time, venture capital firms will also have to spread their wings into these new territories, both in support of their client companies and, eventually, to take advantage of direct investment opportunities in them.

There is, as well, likely to be a substantial increase in the number of growth sectors for venture capital investments, as affluence becomes more widely spread and in order to counter threats to the planet and to its population. Whilst healthcare and technology will continue to be lead sectors, other growth markets are likely to include leisure, tourism, alternative energy, defence, environmental control and security, against threats such as terrorism. All these sectors will, however, need to use advanced technology to stay in the forefront of change.

A third major factor in the marketplace will be the increasing competition that will arise between companies and countries internationally. Companies will need to innovate to stay ahead and countries will all face the same challenge of replacing their declining industries with new ones, both of which will put the spotlight on venture capital. With ever-shortening time scales for the rise and fall of companies, having an effective and resourceful venture capital industry will be vital, particularly in developed areas such as Britain and Continental Europe, which are under the most threat from the emerging territories.

2 Products

Maintaining a creative and fruitful product pipeline will be even more vital in the years ahead, with the increasing pace of change and competition referred to above. It will be important to target this effort carefully to market needs, through specific market research, and to use advances in medical science to reduce the hit and miss nature of some product research and development effort. An example of this is drug development which can be more carefully directed to solve a problem or disease than in the past, because of the far greater knowledge of the human genome.

Technology will also continue to advance on all fronts and will increasingly be applied throughout the economy. The cross-fertilisation of it into growth market sectors will provide exciting investment opportunities.

It will also be necessary to foster relationships between small, entrepreneurial product companies and large market-led players in their industries who can distribute their products. Such relationships will increasingly have to be international.

3 Internationalisation

Advances in electronic communications, such as the Internet, have had and will continue to have a major impact on how business is done and should make it easier for British and Continental European companies to tackle the necessary internationalisation of their products than has previously been the case. Many young people today are more at ease in communicating on the Internet than through the traditional media of face-to-face meetings or the telephone, and this preference will have a major influence on how relationships are established and made to work. A lot of the information required to forge good international partnerships will also be obtained through the Internet, instead of being gathered through direct contact and careful enquiry, as in the past.

Another more negative factor which will have a bearing on international business is the diminishing attraction of air travel, with its costs, risks and tediousness. Such travel is also likely to become under pressure from government and the green lobby, because of its significant effect on global warming.

Lastly, legislation is an increasing obstacle to business within and between countries, and will need to be taken into account and catered for. It will put greater emphasis on trans-national relationships, particularly where forms of protection are practised.

4 People

The number of people wishing either to set up or be part of a young company is likely to go on increasing because of the greater freedoms and satisfactions involved and of the rewards attendant on success. No longer will working for a big company be a ticket for life, as has been the case in the past, and no longer will people have to work in a big city since the Internet overcomes geographical hurdles.

A lot of these new companies will be relatively small and the challenge will be to build them without losing flexibility. Sources of finance will have to be sympathetic to their needs and prepared to invest relatively small amounts of money in order to help get them off the ground.

It is critical that this increasing supply of entrepreneurs and executives should be given help from a vibrant venture capital industry dedicated to help them build successful, export orientated companies. The two developments need to go hand in hand.

All of these changes emphasise the need for an effective venture capital industry in the UK, which is likely to grow in a substantial way in the years ahead, until it becomes comparable in size and importance to the buy-out sector. It is essential that the industry is professional and supportive to the companies that it backs and is a major contributor to their success.

Within this framework of change and development, it is equally essential that the time-honoured commercial values should remain constant and be retained. These include having a focused market strategy, taking a practical approach to product development, organising a company properly with well-motivated staff and, most important of all, having the right attitude to money and its control. Venture capitalists, on their side, must provide the right support and finance, properly structured to meet the needs of the company which they are backing. It is just another case of 'plus ça change, plus c'est la même chose' as far as commercial and venture capital activity is concerned!

TWENTY-SEVEN

THE ROLE OF THE VENTURE CAPITALIST

V ENTURE capital is a long-term investment business in which money is put to work for five to seven years and a venture capitalist has therefore got to be a long-term financial partner for an entrepreneur and the company's managers, which is at the other end of the spectrum to a hedge fund. He must assess the company as having good growth prospects within an existing strategy, management of calibre who are worth backing, and financial projections which can produce a good return on the valuation being offered. Reciprocally, as his enthusiasm for an investment waxes, he has to persuade the company's management team that he can add real value to the business, if he is to get the deal on reasonable terms, often against higher bids. A perceptive entrepreneur and his or her team will want to choose a financial partner who makes a really positive contribution to the development of the business, and will not concentrate solely on maximising the latter's entrance price, but rather will judge him by the size of the cake that he can help to create at the end of the venture capital span.

This added value by the venture capitalist can cover the traditional financial monitoring of a company, assistance in dealing with the hiring and remuneration of executives, genuine help in internationalising the business, and advice on going public or on acquisitions and mergers, both from a buying and a selling standpoint. In order to undertake this role effectively, the venture capitalist must have wide commercial and financial experience since, otherwise, he will not be credible or qualified to deal with the issues involved. A narrower financial capability, whilst relevant to the buy-out business, is not sufficient for the task.

Real venture capital is a difficult business requiring, first, an understanding of markets, products and technologies, second, the ability to judge and work with management and third, a financial expertise, covering both the company and the investment community. When young men or women come to see me, usually with a degree or professional qualification, and say that they want to be a venture capitalist, I tell them to get some business experience. This is not usually what they want to hear, as they are in a hurry to short-cut things and make some capital.

Done properly, and we all have our limitations in this respect, venture capital is a very constructive and satisfying career which can add real value to a business and earn substantial appreciation and respect from entrepreneurs and managers on the receiving end, some of whom will become friends for life. This supportive approach is completely at variance with the somewhat aggressive reputation that venture capital has, in some quarters, of looking after its own interests, rather than that of the investee company. It never ceases to amaze me how high-handed some exponents can be with the sums of money that they manage; it is not even their own money, which probably explains their attitude and behaviour.

I have always been motivated by doing something that is worthwhile, enjoying doing it and seeking to be successful at it. Venture capital is an ideal theatre for such an approach, since nothing is more satisfying than helping to build a company from a small start to become a large international force over a period of years.

I believe that there are parallels between the responsibilities of a venture capitalist and those of a parent. These can start with having a part in the birth of a new company, move on to assisting it through its adolescent years, help bring it to maturity and then encourage it to be independent, once it is finally standing on its own feet. Success in these tasks is achieved when there is an appreciative and harmonious relationship between the two parties, following the company's independence, on the basis that you have to set people free to keep their respect and friendship. Like parents, venture capitalists are less than perfect but, if they

105

do their best and their intentions are good, things usually work out well in the end.

Most successful venture capitalists that I have met are fascinated by their subject and never cease to be excited by interesting propositions that cross their bows. They tend to be low key, down to earth and very direct in their dealings and questions, as well as being modest about their achievements. They also tend, particularly in the US, to stay in the business for a long time, increasingly playing a strategic or grandfather role in the firms that they have helped to create. Longevity brings venture capital experience and perhaps the reverse applies, so that old venture capitalists, like old soldiers, 'never die but just fade away'!

Finally, in all stages of their careers, real venture capitalists, like real entrepreneurs, should be motivated by doing something worthwhile and constructive, thoroughly enjoy doing it and seek to be successful as a measure of performance. Rewards are not the prime object, although they will flow from doing the job properly.

TWENTY-EIGHT

THE ROLE OF THE INVESTOR

I NVESTORS in venture capital have to accept that it is a long-term business in which they are prepared to have their money locked up for up to ten years in return for the expectation of substantial returns. In effect, the lock-up is less in a well-run firm because the money within a ten year fund is called down when needed over the initial three years and paid out to investors as distributions, when realisations are made, normally in the second half of the fund's life.

The returns on individual venture capital investments with a specific company can be spectacular, which raises the profile of the fund and more than makes up for any disappointing investments. In terms of overall fund return, a leading investment bank issued an article, covering the period 1945 to 1993, in which venture capital emerged as the top performing asset class, with an IRR of 16.1% over the forty-eight year period. This figure certainly correlates with my experience over the last thirty years.

Venture capital investors can be individuals who are prepared to act as 'angels' in start-up companies often motivated by the tax breaks available to them. Or they can be individual or institutional investors, with large funds available, who are prepared to invest in a venture capital fund managed by a specialist firm. Such funds normally have a ten year life and involve a spread of investment in specific companies which gives diversification, within a defined policy, for the investor.

Corporate investors are playing an increasing role in venture capital, particularly in the US and Japan, and are usually looking for some commercial spin-off, such as the distribution rights to new products or an inside track as an acquirer, as and when companies in the portfolio come up for sale. It is important that these secondary motives do not adversely impact the fund's primary aim of optimising its return to investors, in these circumstances.

Governments are also taking an increased interest in venture capital but usually their involvements have strings attached, such as an obligation to help create local employment. Such aims, although admirable in themselves, are often counterproductive to the end which they seek to achieve, since they distort the commercial thrust of the fund and subject it, and its investee companies, to bureaucratic and restrictive rules and legislation.

Whatever the category of a venture capital investor, they must have a long-term view and should seek to be supportive of the companies or fund managers that they have chosen, provided that these entities behave properly and do not abuse their trust. Venture capital investors, who are fair-weather friends and short-term in their behaviour, can make the management of a fund very difficult, particularly where they have a large stake.

Good investors, and most of the people and institutions with whom I have worked are in that category, are a pleasure to deal with and are very reasonable, provided that they are properly communicated with and kept informed of any material problems. Whilst they do not like sudden bad surprises, they are normally very supportive of sensible solutions for dealing with problems.

Much of the money in UK private equity goes into the buy-out field because of the returns achieved in recent years in that sector. I believe, however, that institutions need to put more money into real venture capital, partly because the buy-out market is over-crowded and faces more difficult trading conditions and partly because the prospects for venture capital are very good. In particular, the healthcare and technology markets offer high growth prospects in an investment arena where growth is going to be increasingly difficult to come by.

With greater investor support to the venture capital sector, more young men and women of talent will be attracted into it and will be prepared to put in the groundwork of building-up their skills and experience in order to become effective in the sector. With time, it should be possible to develop a strong cadre of real venture capital companies in the UK, as has happened previously in the US.

Over the last thirty years during my time in venture capital, institutions have moved from being prepared to take risks and making their own judgements to playing safe in order to avoid exposure, often sub-contracting the role of private equity investment to fund of funds managers and investment consultants. The whole process has become over-analytical and bureaucratic and has resulted in a situation where it is very difficult to 'see the wood for the trees'.

The net effect of all this is that more and more money goes into the conventional thinking of what has performed in the recent past and what is seen to be fashionable, which led to the dot-com disaster of the late 1990s and has now led to a huge over-investment in the buy-out business, particularly in the UK. The latter is getting increasingly exposed, as deal prices go up and the economic environment for investee companies became more difficult, as in the retail sector. Anyone with a long memory, will remember the major recession that was sparked by this type of activity in the early 1970s when interest rates rose and equity values fell.

The rigours of due diligence in institutions and their advisers (with its emphasis on analysis and system) often undertaken by young people with limited commercial experience, are no substitute for seasoned judgement, taking into account future conditions as well as past performance. The Roman god, Janus, had two heads, one looking to the future and one looking to the past, with hopefully equal weighting.

It sometimes seems that the only people nowadays prepared to back their own judgement are private investors or family trusts which have not yet become institutionalised. They are, in addition, prepared to take a longer-term view because they are not subject to the quarterly treadmill applied to investment managers by the pressures of the market, and by corporate governance.

An extraordinary situation has arisen in which the largest potential investors in venture capital are antagonistic to risk which, as explored earlier, is implicit in that type of activity. Classically today, institutional investors and their advisers are loathe to back a first fund of a new manager but are interested in follow-on funds, if the first is successful. Such an approach, applied to investee companies by venture capital firms, would mean that no new start-ups would ever be invested in by them!

Investors, particularly institutional ones, should seek to rebuild direct relationships with venture capital firms, and should be less dependent on outside intermediaries. They should be far less preoccupied with size, since this inhibits the sector's development and makes the whole process antagonistic to enterprise. It also means that they miss out on some sparkling returns, particularly where an acorn grows into an oak tree.

Twenty-Nine

The Impact on the Economy

T HE PRIME objective of real venture capital is to produce good and fast expanding companies in high growth industries, such as healthcare and technology. These companies, which normally have a high export thrust and weighting, are of vital importance to the UK economy, preoccupied as it is with backing and recycling the ownership of mature companies, coupled with an ever-increasing investment in state-sponsored organisations.

With so many of the lower technology products and jobs being moved off-shore to low-cost areas such as China and India, it is vital that new high value and margin businesses should be created, with the beneficial effect that they have on the trade balance, jobs, taxes and general national confidence. In this context, we need to create the Glaxos of tomorrow and not allow British innovation and technology to be taken over and exploited by foreign corporations and sources of finance. Britain has a good reputation as a fertile source of ideas and inventions, particularly in science and technology, but a poor one in its ability to exploit these strengths in a commercially successful way.

The role of venture capital is a vital one in changing this and helping to reverse the decline of British industry. For this to happen, the country's resources must be concentrated more on important longer-term developments and less on short-term financial profits, often achieved on very uninteresting companies with a limited future.

This regeneration will require a substantial reorientation of private equity funding and, in particular, a preparedness by institutions to put a higher proportion of their money into real venture capital, as proposed earlier. Governments should also help by concentrating on creating the right climate for enterprise and not try to interfere in the process, since its direct involvement is usually a disadvantage. True entrepreneurs want support and encouragement but are passionate about being able to stand on their own feet and being free of unnecessary constraint.

The role of Government mentioned above is vital in achieving the objectives outlined and, in particular, in helping to develop new growth companies. Its main contribution must be to create a climate which is favourable to young companies and frees them from the bureaucratic and regulatory burdens which are so stultifying to enterprise. Within this more encouraging frame-work, there is, in our Utopian world, scope for some specific action, such as:

- favourable treatment of exports
- R&D grants for genuine technology products and inventions
- less onerous capital gains tax for new companies
- investor incentives targeted towards real venture capital.

Attempts have already been made by Government to cover some of these areas but these need to be reviewed, so that they are focused to help genuine growth companies, which can make a substantial contribution to the nation's future. The aim must be to attract more talent and money into that arena and into real venture capital since, at the moment, its rewards and risks compare unfavourably to those prevalent in other fields such as large companies, investment banking and the public sector.

The impact of a greater emphasis on real venture capital, coupled with positive action from the Government in some of the areas mentioned, will take time to make itself felt. However, a beginning has to be made to set events in train and a successful outcome is likely to be demonstrated, in economic terms, by:

- an increase in the number of start-up companies, both out of universities and elsewhere, which adopt a commercial approach from an early stage and which are therefore attractive from a funding standpoint

112

- a determination by founders of companies to develop their potential and not to sell out at the first opportunity, and a recognition by them that, with the right help, they can continue to achieve well
- success in these first two steps, and an equal – if not greater – determination by these founders and their teams to build a big business and become an international force, again with the right help.

The job of building a business is an onerous one and, if the task can be made easier with genuine assistance in areas which are new to the entrepreneur concerned, he or she is more likely to persevere with the task for longer, on the basis that it is less stressful and therefore more enjoyable. Like learning how to swim, it is more fun if you receive positive assistance over a period of time rather than being thrown in at the deep end at the outset!

THIRTY

CONCLUSIONS AND LESSONS

THE FIRST main conclusion, stemming from the ground covered in this book, is that real venture capital is a very important sector which has a vital role to fulfil, although it is, admittedly, a difficult one to do well.

The right approach to venture capital must be to ensure that a growth company has a focused strategy for its markets and products, has good management and a heavy emphasis on profit and cash flow in order to build up a strong balance sheet and a self-financing business.

It is imperative that opportunities should be sought in high growth international markets, of which the lead ones are health-care and technology. This enhances the upside of an investment and reduces its risk, since the currents are flowing in a favourable direction.

Within these markets, such opportunities should involve the commercial application of products and technologies to meet clearly defined customer needs. The aim of the exercise must be to make money and technology must be seen as a means to an end, rather than an end in itself.

Moving to the tactical aspects of an investment, it is crucial to back high quality entrepreneurs and managers who have commercial flair, get things done and are trustworthy. It is also crucial to have a strong financial function in the company and to have confidence in its financial figures and reporting system, which is sometimes difficult in a young company.

The financing of suitable venture capital investments should be kept simple and should be orientated to fostering growth, which is generally best achieved through the use of ordinary shares or common stock. Where gearing is introduced, it should be limited and be logically based, either to enable management to buy shares at a price it can afford or to meet the terms of the deal with regard to equity dilution or valuation.

Once a business has been established in its home market, attention should be turned to exploiting the potential of its products internationally in order to give it a wide market spread. Such international niche businesses provide for continuing organic growth and, from an investment standpoint, can combine high reward with relatively low risk. The international development and financing of these businesses are difficult tasks but ones on which an experienced venture capital partner can make a major contribution.

Intuitive judgement is vital in selecting investments, but it must be backed up by relevant tactical data collected through searching due diligence. Disciplined investment processes must be applied to this and other aspects of the investment cycle, within a well managed venture capital firm.

Future developments and changes in the economic and commercial environment should have a beneficial effect on venture capital and make it even more important as a sector. It is vital, therefore, that a professional and efficient venture capital industry is built up in the UK.

People going into venture capital have got to be prepared to build up the right experience beforehand. Only thus can they be of genuine help to entrepreneurs and managers on a partnership basis in which they add substantial value to the business.

The role of a venture capitalist, properly executed, is a very constructive one since he or she is using his or her training and experience to assist the business in areas which may be new to its executives. Examples of this could be internationalisation, acquisition, flotation and trade sale, in addition to the more routine tasks of being on a Board and monitoring an investment.

Venture capitalists must concentrate on helping to build really exciting and sound companies which can successfully be floated to everyone's advantage and satisfaction. In this, they must resist the temptation to take on and float short-term or unsound propositions, which not only give venture capital and their investee companies a bad name but also result in a loss of confidence in the high growth sectors involved.

Against this background, investing institutions have got to be more discriminating about the policies of the venture capital firms that they back, so that a higher proportion of their funds goes into real venture capital. This will ultimately be to everyone's advantage, including their own, and certainly will also be in the national interest.

The purpose of this book has been to argue the case for real venture capital and to encourage more people of talent to go into it, once they have built up the requisite experience to be able to help companies. Like entrepreneurs, they should be motivated by the idea of helping to create really exciting companies, rather than feathering their own nests and, if they do this well, they will find that their own interests are taken care of, as a consequence of success.

I have spent thirty years in venture capital and the first lesson that I have learnt is not to be talked out of one's instincts by someone who claims to be certain that he or she is right. Invariably, in my experience, such confidence is not to be relied upon.

A second lesson is not to work with people who do not reciprocate, since all successful relationships are dependent upon 'give and take'. Pick people who are generous spirited and good team players.

A third lesson is to adopt the philosophy that there is no limit to what you can achieve, as long as you do not mind who gets the credit. There will be no shortage of claimants!

Other supporting conclusions and lessons which reinforce these points are:

- do not back people with a different attitude to money, since the relationship is unlikely to be a fruitful one and will probably end in tears
- be financially conservative, albeit being prepared to take calculated risks when opportunities present themselves
- do not think that you can change people fundamentally, since all you can do is to help them be aware of, rather than alter, their strengths and weaknesses
- do not overgear companies since it constrains their growth and increases their vulnerability, and avoid gearing altogether in early-stage companies.

116

- do not fall in love with technology but concentrate on the scope for its practical and commercial application
- do not go for low growth sectors, since they have inadequate upside for real venture capital
- remember that strategy is relatively easy, if you can think, but tactics and timing are difficult
- be imaginative but remember that 'imagination can be the mistress of illusion'
- lastly, from an entrepreneur's standpoint, make sure that venture capitalists (who say that they are hands-on) have the requisite experience to play such a role. Do reciprocal due diligence on them, prior to an investment.

In all of this, it should be remembered that the aim of real venture capital is to help create Derby winners rather than good hunters, which are already well-served by other sectors of the private equity field. Such an outcome requires a lot of effort, over a protracted period of time, and is ultimately well worth it, both in satisfaction and financial rewards.

An Early Paper on Venture Capital

Introduction

Venture capital was originally the term applied to the financing of new ventures but it has subsequently been extended to the provision of finance for turnround situations and for the development of companies prior to their becoming clearing bank propositions. The wider interpretation, biased heavily to small companies, is used in this paper on venture capital which was first written by myself in March 1977 prior to the formation of Thompson Clive & Partners Limited in that year, and secondly updated in February 1984 as the material for a presentation to the National Association of Pension Funds Conference at Eastbourne.

The paper begins with some definitions, reviews the background and history of venture capital in the UK, examines the current situation and structure of the industry, analyses the shortcomings of traditional approaches and forecasts how future patterns are likely to develop in the country. It ends with a summary of what are seen to be the keys to success in venture capital investment.

The original paper was based upon a limited amount of research, both because of time constraints and the dearth of published information in 1977. The updated paper had the advantage of being able to draw upon statistics in the industry which had become available by then.

In general, the facts presented in this paper, although inevitably incomplete, are considered to provide a sufficient foundation for the conclusions and views which follow them.

Definitions

Within the general definition given in the introduction, there are four key characteristics to venture capital namely:

- there must be a potential equity participation
- the investment should be a long-term one, usually in the range five to ten years
- there should be an active participation from the investor, both in terms of money and expertise
- this participation should continue through all stages until the company can attract conventional financial support from financial institutions or the stock market.

Much venture capital is therefore concerned with helping emergent companies through their various stages of evolution, and high risk should be limited to start-ups and turnrounds. Even on these it can be argued that the risk is mitigated by the fact that the venture capitalist and his backers are usually in a position to take action when things go wrong, which is of course not an option in a normal stockmarket or other arms-length investment.

The interrelationship between venture and development capital is an important one although somewhat difficult to be precise about. In general, venture capital is concerned with emergent companies, as discussed, whereas development capital is concerned with mature companies which have an established market and product position; in reality of course the dividing line is blurred with many companies having a mix of the emergent and the mature in their make-up. Another way of looking at the problem is that venture capital is concerned with early-phase financing until the company is established as a going concern and development capital with later-phase financing against a profit record, although in practice there is again overlap between the two stages.

Background and History

The availability of venture and development capital to the small private company sector in the UK has not always kept pace with demand in this country. In the past this was due to the increasing incidence of taxation on wealthy individuals and the development of an easily accessible market in quoted securities. Savings that might otherwise have been invested in private companies were diverted into quoted investments.

This problem was serious enough in 1930 to result in the establishment of the Macmillan Committee which identified a gap in the supply of funds available to support small company growth and rationalisation. This Committee proposed the creation of a company to devote itself to the provision of such funds.

In response to the Macmillan Report there appeared a number of investment institutions specialising in the financing of small firms. However, the combined resources of these companies were limited and only part of the demand could be satisfied.

The Industrial and Commercial Finance Corporation (ICFC), which was created in 1945 by a consortium of clearing banks with support from the Bank of England, was the first major initiative in the field of venture and development capital. Not only was ICFC first into the field, certainly in the post-war period, but the scale of its operations dwarfs the rest of the UK venture capital industry with it currently having over £480 million invested in 3,900 or so businesses paving the way for venture capital in the UK.

The National Research Development Corporation (NRDC) was established by the Government under the Development of Inventions Act 1948 specifically to provide finance for the development of innovations, particularly those originating outside industry. Thus NRDC was set up primarily to back projects rather than companies.

The Ratcliffe Committee, reporting in 1959, discussed the adequacy of the provision of finance for small firms entirely with reference to ICFC and the joint stock banks. They were satisfied that the capital gap, in the terms of the Macmillan formulation, had been closed by ICFC but their report contained recommendations which resulted in:

- the provision of term loans by the joint stock banks
- the ending of a formal upper limit on the size of ICFC's investment
- the creation of Technical Development Capital Limited (TDC) to finance small and very small firms involved in exploiting a technical innovation.

TDC has now of course become the venture capital arm of ICFC which is itself part of the Investors in Industry Group.

In the mid 1960s City institutions became increasingly interested in venture capital and in technology, stemming from the success of the American Research and Development Corporation (ARD) and its investment in Digital Equipment. They also became increasingly interested in investment in unquoted companies and a number of venture capital departments were set up.

The electronics sector was in fashion in the mid 1960s and the very high Price/Earnings ratios available in this sector, and hence the prospect of floating other electronics companies at high P/E ratios, was a strong attraction to the venture capital community. At this time, a number of investments were made in electronics companies which in some instances not only failed to provide the desired capital gains but also led to substantial losses.

Venture capital investment in the late 1960s and early 1970s got caught up in the property boom of that time and the asset stripping era that developed from it. As a result, many venture capital propositions were asset orientated and high geared, on the basis that substantial profits could be earned by the equity shareholders once a successful deal or series of deals had been carried out. The scope for this came to an end with the collapse of the property boom and several venture capital organisations were caught up in its vortex.

Venture capital reached its nadir in the mid 1970s when there seemed little scope for achieving dramatic returns on investment either through earnings growth or asset dealing. The combination of recession and high interest rates dramatically reduced the attractions of venture capital investments and, what industrial investment there was, tended to be in safer and dividend paying mature companies which looked well set to weather the storm.

In the latter half of the 1970s, Equity Capital for Industry and the National Enterprise Board were set up to provide venture and development finance, the first with the support of some financial institutions and the second with that of the Labour Government. ECI is of course still independent but the NEB has been merged with the NRDC under the new umbrella of the British Technology Group.

Since the late 1970s the climate has progressively improved, culminating in a boom in UK venture capital at the present time. The reasons for this and the structure of the industry which has evolved are examined in the next section.

Current Situation and Structure

The seeds of the current boom in venture capital in the UK were laid with the election of the Thatcher Government in May 1979. Whilst the Government was in its early years heavily pre-occupied with monetary and economic problems, it did restore the importance of profitability in the public mind and it also gave encouragement to emerging technologies and companies which could contribute to new wealth creation in the economy. Initially such encouragement was of a general nature but took more concrete form through the launch of the Business Start-Up Scheme (BSS) in 1981 and the Business Expansion Scheme (BES) in 1983, which transformed the tax legislation in the UK and made it very favourable to venture capital and associated forms of investment.

The second major factor leading to the current situation is of course the microchip which has had a major impact on venture capital, both here and in the US. It has produced a spate of opportunities in rapidly growing markets and there have been some dramatic investment successes, and it has also produced a new breed of entrepreneur whose prime strength lies in his understanding and leadership in a particular sphere of tech-nology. Only recently has some of the gilt begun to fall off the gingerbread, as competition in the computer industry hots up and reasonably priced deals become scarce.

The third and final factor bearing on the current situation has been the buoyancy of the Unlisted Securities Market (USM), established in 1980, and of the Stock Market. Both markets have shown a considerable appetite for new issues, particularly in high technology companies, and there has been a flow of such flotations in the last three years.

In this favourable environment the venture capital industry in the UK has expanded very rapidly and there has been a proliferation of new venture capital companies and funds. Since 1979 the number of venture capital concerns operating in the UK has multiplied threefold from nineteen to sixty, made up broadly of the following categories:

- publicly listed investment companies specialising in venture capital
- private venture capital companies such as Thompson Clive
- offshoots of US venture capital companies
- business start-up and expansion scheme funds
- captive venture capital subsidiaries of banks etc.
- other venture capital investors such as ICFC which still dwarfs the rest of the industry.

Between 1979 and the end of September 1983, fifty-one new funds were launched and £281 million was committed to independent venture capital companies. 1981 was a peak year for new venture capital company and fund formation due to it being the year in which:

- the Stock Exchange introduced new listing requirements for investment companies, resulting in the formation of five new concerns
- the Government introduced the Business Start-Up Scheme which led to the formation of eleven new funds managing £25 million
- the improved environmental conditions, and particularly the establishment of the USM at the end of

the previous year, first encouraged a number of independent companies, some with US links, to go out and raise money for venture capital investment.

The growth continued in 1982 and 1983, with the main emphasis on independent venture capital companies. However, an increasing number of City institutions already experienced in portfolio investment has become interested in venture capital, particularly since the introduction of the Business Expansion Scheme in 1983. Nineteen approved BES funds were set up in that year to raise £30 million and of these no less than ten, or even half, are being, or will be, managed by merchant banks, stockbrokers, investment trust managers or other financial advisors.

Of the fifty-one new funds raised for venture capital between 1979 and September 1983, six were new funds floated in the Stock Exchange, twenty-four were private with mainly institutional backing and twenty-one were BSS/BES funds. By the end of 1983, the BSS/BES total had risen to thirty.

Of the £281 million raised by independent venture capital concerns, £108 million was provided through the Stock Market. The remaining £173 million relating to private venture capital concerns was primarily provided by financial institutions, with pension funds providing the lead share of £34.4 million or 19.8%. Until recently, very little money was provided by private individuals, although this situation is changing dramatically.

Turning to the way in which these and previous funds were deployed, it is estimated that between the beginning of 1981 and the middle of 1983, £170 million was invested in UK companies, £37 million in US companies and £3.5 million in Continental companies.

In the UK, about one third of the money invested was in start-ups, one third in expansion finance and one third in management buyouts. Regionally, 85% was deployed in England, 10% in Scotland and 5% in Wales.

In industry sector terms, 19% of the funds invested went into computer related companies, 18% into communications and other electronic companies and 14% into genetic engineering and healthcare companies. In total about 50% of investment was into technology orientated companies.

Traditional Approaches and Problems

Venture capital is by its nature a difficult business in which a minority investment is normally made without asset cover or yield expectation with the object of achieving a sizeable capital gain in due course. Success depends very heavily on reading correctly the earnings prospects of the company, often with no previous track record, and on the climate for realising the investment when it comes good, either through flotation or sale.

It was seen earlier that the venture capital industry in the UK has had its ups and downs in the past and it is important that careful stock be taken of the shortcomings of previous approaches and of some of the problems, where they were experienced. Otherwise, there is a danger that the cycle will repeat itself with damaging results to the industry and to investor confidence, particularly where expectations have become unrealistic.

In the past, questions have been raised about the level of finance available for the smaller company. Few such questions are being asked at the present time when there is, if anything, a surfeit of funds in search of good propositions, particularly in the fashionable high technology areas. Too much money, can, however, be as ruinous to a young company as it can be to a young person and can erode the sturdy, fighting spirit that is necessary in competitive markets, and most successful venture capital start-ups in the UK are short on finance and long on toil and sweat.

The motives behind the provision of finance are also important since most venture capital situations require careful and painstaking support over several years and a preparedness on the part of the investors to help the company concerned through its growing pains and other problems. Understanding parents are necessary if an adolescent is to grow into a mature and responsible adult, and equally investors should not have unrealistic expectations for their company offspring, nor be unduly alarmed by the set backs which will inevitably arise.

A new dimension which has emerged in venture capital financing is the BSS and BES funds, which have somewhat different financial aims and pressures to the classical venture capital approach. They do bring the private investor back into the venture capital arena which is a very good thing but there must be some concern at the pressure they are under to invest, the rate of which is approximately three to four times that of a normal fund.

Turning from finance to the venture capital skills required to invest and administer it, there has in the past been too strong a financial bias in the teams involved and not enough industrial expertise, particularly on the technological or marketing fronts. This has sometimes led to faulty and too subjective assessments of situations and particularly of technologies, products and markets; in venture capital it is the intangible assets rather than the tangible assets that matter.

Whilst recent attempts have been made to achieve a fusion of financial and industrial skills, it is difficult to bring about the right balance of people suited to and experienced in dealing with small companies. As the funds under management grow there is also an inevitable process for the team to become increasingly financial, with industrial experience often limited to the accounting function, and there is every prospect of history repeating itself in the present situation. Equally dangerous of course to a finance organisation which does not understand industry is an industrial organisation which does not understand finance.

Looking at the past, it can be argued that the real shortage has been not of money but of the entrepreneurs and opportunities available for backing. In the short term the microchip has had a significant impact on this issue, as discussed earlier, but the real question is whether in the longer term the greater supply of finance will bring out more entrepreneurs and opportunities from other sectors of the economy. Clearly it would be unhealthy for all or the bulk of new development to be concentrated on one sector of the economy, exciting though that sector is.

It is important that the thinking relating to the assessment of opportunities should be intelligent, realistic and flexible and that the temptation in particular to copy the American model of venture capital here should be avoided. The reasons for this are primarily that the home market base for emerging companies is much smaller in the UK than in the US and that the rapid and massive organic growth often experienced there is not possible here. The risks of course are also usually less which is important since UK investors are less attuned to writing-off investments than US ones.

Whilst it may take longer to help a UK company grow, once it is established then the secondary financing of international market expansion and possibly acquisition is very important and often vital to its achieving a mature and viable stance. Institutions should therefore be prepared to shrug off any early set backs and frustrations and help good companies through this vital phase in which the quality and quantity of finance are of paramount importance.

Future Patterns and Solutions

If history both here and in the US is anything to go by, the recent rapid expansion in venture capital in the UK is likely to be followed by a period of shake-out when some of the unrealistic expectations which exist are not fulfilled and some of the inevitable failures start coming through. At that time, it is vital that the leading financial institutions, particularly the pension funds and insurance companies, should continue to give a lead and to remain committed to venture capital and to the essential follow-up development capital finance.

Such a shake-out must, however, be viewed as a short-term correction only to the growth of a vital industry which itself needs to become mature. The venture capital organisations which emerge, though possibly smaller in number than at present, are likely to be very professional and experienced and to play a genuine role with the client companies, even on occasion taking direct responsibility for a company to see it through a particular problem. Any successful venture capital concern will need to harmonise under its umbrella the different skills and cultures of the financial and industrial worlds, and to be equally at home dealing with its institutional backers and the managements of the companies in which it is invested.

Turning to investment opportunities, the computer-related and other electronics industries will obviously continue to be growth sectors, although they will become more competitive and more vulnerable to swings in consumer spending. Other sectors of industry will also need to be opened up, either where there is scope for rapid technological advance in an established industry or where there are good long-term growth prospects, as in healthcare or leisure spending.

Although start-ups will continue to be the classical 'rags to riches' success story in venture capital, there will be increasing opportunities in the years ahead for management buy-outs under which subsidiaries of large Groups are spun out and given a new and independent lease of life. The attractions of such buy-outs will increase in harsh times when investors tend to go for safer and often dividend paying companies, particularly where there is not a buoyant stock market providing a flotation prospect.

Management buy-outs are not without their problems and the companies spun out often need more than money. However, they can be very fruitful for all parties, not least of all the selling Group which is able to concentrate on its main business; indeed it can be argued that large companies would be better off having venture capital investments as in the US rather than owning direct subsidiaries peripheral to their main businesses.

Management buy-outs can also help create a climate in which executives are more prepared to have a go and to become more enterprising. A supply of such entrepreneurs is clearly going to be vital in the years ahead if there are going to be enough good people and opportunities to back.

The combination from a venture capital point of view of new venture financing, development financing and management buy-outs is an attractive one with obvious overlap between the three, and is particularly suited to the UK which can be less sure of consistent long-term growth than for instance the West Coast of America. It provides an acceptable balance both of reward and risk and of capital gain and income.

Looking to the longer term, it is vital that the emphasis in favour of the smaller company should be maintained, although it must not be forgotten that the object is to make small companies big both for growth reasons and in order to make up for those big companies which are likely to become small or even to cease to exist. There are likely to be considerable opportunities for smaller companies in the years ahead as markets and technologies change and the need for innovation, speed and flexibility of response increases.

The venture capital industry has a critical role to play in this process, as have the financial institutions in providing the essential finance.

Keys to Success

The ingredients required for a flourishing venture capital business in a country can be summarised as:

- a favourable political, fiscal and social climate
- a ready supply of finance
- motivated entrepreneurs, producing a flow of opportunities
- qualified venture capitalists
- exit vehicles.

All these ingredients exist in the UK at the present time.

Within this positive framework, it is vital that specific investments are made as professionally as possible and the keys to success in this are seen to be as follows:

1   *The Opportunity*
    The best opportunities are those which have been worked up over a period of time, often starting with a personal introduction, rather than those which are cold canvasses through the mail. The venture capitalist undoubtedly has a responsibility to take his wares to the market rather than wait in this office for the world to come to him.

2   *The Market and the Product*
    The market in which the company is engaged should offer scope for high growth and the prospect of high margins over at least a five year term ahead. There will be variants of this, for instance when a company has the opportunity to

increase substantially its market share in a more stagnant market, although these should be an exception.

Turning to the product, clearly it must be proven and should ideally be the leader in its field with some protection either through patents or more normally through 'know-how', for instance in the software behind a computer systems business.

The venture capitalist should know the market and product areas in which he is working, and specialisation is therefore vital in his business. He should also be able to mount at short notice the resources to carry out due diligence on the company, including in particular research on its market and its product.

3   *The Management*

Some people make money and some people do not, and the key judgement of any would-be entrepreneur must be of his commercial acumen. Many successful entrepreneurs are difficult to deal with and tend to be a law unto themselves but are often worth persevering with if they produce results.

As a company becomes larger and moves from a product to a market led phase, a more disciplined and professional approach to management becomes necessary. This is usually achieved by broadening the base of the management team or on occasion by bringing in a new chairman or managing director.

The relationship between the venture capitalist and the management is a crucial one that ideally should bring the marriage of complementary skills. It does, however, need careful fostering and usually achieves fruition when problems have been surmounted together and a full understanding has been reached in the heat of the battle.

4   *The Finance*

Last and in some ways least comes the provision of finance. The best venture capital investments are often those in which the company concerned needs very little money, for instance either in a low capitalisation start-up or in the purchase of shares from a founder who needs funds more than the company does. Obviously in the development capital phase the situation changes dramatically and substantial funds are required to fuel expansion.

The standard venture capital ratio is to seek to achieve a multiple of at least five times the initial investment within five years, based on the American model. In practice in any venture capital portfolio of, say, ten there will normally be two investments which greatly exceed this target, six which achieve a respectable return short of it and two which fail to perform. The impact of successes is usually, however, very much greater than that of failures, and can transform the value of a portfolio.

Before providing finance, the venture capitalist must carry out proper due diligence on a company and, where significant sums are involved, should ensure that proper accounting and legal investigations have been conducted on the company.

5   *Implementation*

The venture capitalist should normally have one or possibly two part-time directors on the Board of the company, depending on the size of the stake taken. His object is to play a positive role to help the company forward and this can involve raising further finance, identifying product licences or acquisitions and making international connections. The better the company does the more positive and fruitful the relationship normally becomes.

However, if things go badly wrong, the venture capitalist must be prepared to intervene to protect his and his syndicate partners' investment who together may control the company. He must also of course be capable of intervention and industrial expertise is again vital in this regard.

The venture capitalist should therefore have a double-barrelled strategy of positively backing successes but having a fall-back solution to failures. He should not seek intervention but should be prepared to undertake it, if it is necessary.

In conclusion, it must be stressed that venture capital is a difficult and demanding business but a worthwhile one which can produce returns well in excess of more traditional forms of investment. Investors must, however, be prepared to be patient and persevering in the resolution of problems in any given business and should essentially take a long-term view of their involvements.

THE HEALTHCARE AND TECHNOLOGY MARKETS

This Appendix sets out the profiles of the healthcare and technology markets with a view to highlighting their attractiveness for venture capital investment. Both markets are very large, have good long-term growth prospects and are truly international. In each case, they are dominated, from a size and investment standpoint, by the United States.

The bulk of this Appendix was, as mentioned in the main text, prepared for a lecture that I gave on International Venture Capital in 1999 at the Tuck School of Management at Dartmouth College, New Hampshire. Whilst the figures and much of the material are out-of-date, the fundamental characteristics and investment potential of the markets portrayed are broadly unchanged.

1 The Healthcare Market

The healthcare market has annual revenue in excess of US$1 trillion and the US share of this is estimated at about 40% with an annual growth rate of 11%, based on figures for the largest sector, pharmaceuticals.

The market is made up of a number of sectors of which the following are now explored:

- Pharmaceuticals
- Biotechnology
- Medical Devices
- Health Information

1.1   Pharmaceuticals

The global pharmaceutical industry has annual sales in the region of US$190 billion and an annual research and development spend of US$35 billion. Over the past year, sales have grown 11% in North America and 6% in Europe, its two leading markets.

The pharmaceutical sector is an attractive area for investment because it is large and international and has the essential ingredient of long-term growth due, on the one hand, to expanding and ageing populations and, on the other, to a trend towards the prevention rather than the cure of diseases. For instance, it is sensible and cheaper to treat high blood pressure through the use of drugs in order to reduce the incidence of strokes and heart attacks, with their consequent serious social and medical implications.

The sector is dominated by a number of large blue-chip pharma companies which, in the main, are commercially strong and successful and provide an ideal customer base for many smaller healthcare companies providing support services. Furthermore, the market is fragmented with no one company dominating the sector and even giants like Glaxo and Merck have market shares of less than 10% each, with other major companies having less than 5% each. This situation is likely to change in the future as consolidation in the sector gathers momentum.

Traditionally drug discovery, which has been the prime function of pharma companies, has been an expensive, time consuming and unpredictable affair with a drug, on average, costing about US$380 million to develop and taking about twelve years to reach the market from discovery. A large number of drugs, the overriding majority, fall by the wayside and only about one in three of those that survive recoup their original development costs.

Pharma companies are, therefore, very dependent on a narrow base of successful drugs which have a limited protected life, before they are subject to competition from generic compounds. The situation is aggravated by the fact that a large proportion of the patented period for a drug is eroded by the regulatory and approval cycle. Because of this, companies are under continual pressure to come up with a blockbuster drug which will replace or supplement its older products, with such a step being easier said than done, due to the unpredictable nature of drug discovery.

In the 1980's the major pharma companies built up, in the wake of a very prosperous period for them, large fixed overheads to cater for the high demands which they were experiencing. As the commercial environment became tougher in the early 1990's, with government restrictions and price controls and the expansion of cost-conscious HMOs, a move developed for them to outsource a number of their activities and convert these fixed overheads to variable costs, which they would have more control over.

The first wave of outsourcing involved the formation of a number of contract research organisations (CROs) who offered services to pharma companies on a contract basis. These services involved assistance through Phases I–III of the drug testing cycle, and comprised carrying out trials, collecting and analysing clinical data and obtaining regulatory approval for a drug from the Federal Drug Administration (FDA) or other regulatory authority. The larger CROs set out to offer a full service to pharma companies, covering everything from pre-clinical to Phase III on an international basis and, as a result, became substantial companies in their own right. The industry took off in the early 1990s and a number of market leaders emerged, some of whom went public on NASDAQ and other major exchanges.

As the CRO industry matured, a number of its leading companies developed strategic alliances with pharma companies, covering periods of at least five years, and this enabled both parties to plan ahead and develop complementary resources and facilities. They were, therefore, often able to develop large backlogs of orders from their clients which helped their commercial stability and confidence in, for instance, going public.

However, being labour intensive, CROs found it necessary to expand their staff to cope with added demand and, in the process, had to build up their own fixed costs, albeit in a specialist area. Attempts to look for products to be sold with services, in order to escape the cost escalation treadmill, only had limited success.

The basis of the outsourcing to CROs was that the new wave of these companies would be able to manage their specialist resources more effectively and, as a result, reduce the time taken to bring a drug to market. Any shortening of the regulatory process clearly has a major commercial benefit for a pharma company and, in the main, the outsourcing worked well.

Following on from this trend, the pharma companies helped in the creation of Contract Sales Organisations(CSOs) which were formed to provide 'commando' sales forces to help launch new drugs, leaving the client's existing sales forces to concentrate on their main-line products and not be distracted by new products. The main function of the CSO was to make a success, from a sales point of view, of a new product launch and take the drug to a point where it was established and could be taken over by the pharma company's own sales force. Sometimes, CSOs were used at the other end of the spectrum and asked to inject new life and impetus into drugs that were tired and tailing off, although this was very much a subsidiary role.

Another area of sub-contracted services is now offered by the Contract Communications Organisations (CCOs) which provide strategic marketing services to pharma companies, usually in connection with the launch of a new drug. They specialise in doing the market planning for the new launch and prepare all the editorial and support literature required for the new product, as well as arranging conferences for the medical fraternity in order to inform and enthuse them about the new drug and its capabilities, together with details of its most suitable use and applications.

As the outsourcing industry grew and matured, CROs looked at ways of extending their services to clients and some amalgamations took place in which they acquired CSOs and CCOs. Whilst this gave a wider offering of services, it was important not to lose the values of specialisation on which the outsourcing movement was founded.

Another development in the industry has been the advances in genomics and other allied sciences, which enable a much more scientific approach to be taken to the drug discovery and development process. This has led to the formation of a number of small drug discovery companies which are able to provide services to pharma companies and assist them in the management of their development process. In theory, some of these small companies should be able to undertake drug discovery on their own account in time, since the days of needing to be big in order to develop a new drug should be numbered, with a more targeted and rationale approach being possible.

With these changes, the role of pharma companies will increasingly be to control the R&D process, but not necessarily undertake all their drug discovery and development in house. They are likely also to continue to major on the global distribution of their own and licensed products, since their distribution capability is one of their great strengths.

In summary, the main opportunities for venture capital investment in the pharmaceutical sector are in services companies rather than in pharma ones which are far too big and established entities. This situation could gradually change in the future as drug discovery becomes more precise and as its techniques becomes more prevalent, so that only a relatively small amount of capital is required in the sector, particularly with companies that start by offering discovery and development services. Many of all these categories of services companies, which swim in the wake of large pharma, provide excellent investment opportunities, since they combine revenue growth, profitability, good cash flow and often have large order backlogs, stretching out over several years.

1.2   Biotechnology

The biotechnology sector is at the other end of the spectrum to the pharmaceutical one since most of the companies in it have no revenues or profits and have adverse cash flows and weak balance sheets which need constant recharging as losses are incurred, often over a five to ten year time span. It does, however, have a strong pipeline of prospective products and is responsible for about 25% of the combined pharmaceutical and biotechnology R&D spend.

Whilst biotechnology companies are usually more entrepreneurial and faster moving than their pharma cousins, due to their smaller size and lower overheads, they are often vulnerable with heavy dependence on a few key scientists or people and a similar dependence upon the appetite of investors for high risk investment which can be unprofitable for long periods. Risks are compounded by the uncertainty and protracted length of the regulatory approval period, although rewards can be substantial where new product breakthroughs occur.

With their concentration on the drug discovery and development process and their financing limitations, biotechnology companies are heavily dependent on help from the CRO industry in order to avoid the build-up of unnecessary fixed costs, and some CROs seek to accommodate them by charging reduced fees combined with equity options or stakes to give themselves a profit incentive in the enterprises that they are helping develop. Similarly, biotech companies are very reliant on big pharma for help in the initial distribution of their products, once Phase III approval has been obtained, and increasingly such alliances will be good for both sets of companies, with biotech companies needing marketing muscle and pharma ones needing new products. Relationships between the two can either continue on an arms-length basis or can involve a strategic minority investment by the pharma company or can lead to an outright acquisition, depending on price and the wishes of both parties. Such acquisitions by pharma companies are likely to increase substantially in the years ahead, due to the complementary nature of the biotech and pharma industries and to their mutual dependence.

Investment in the biotech industry is not for the faint-hearted since opportunities are inevitably high-cap ones which require a lot of faith and patience over a number of years, during which time the financial attractions of the industry can ebb and flow. An example if this was in the early 1990s in which period the expectations for biotech companies were hyped and the market had a major set-back when performance was disappointing. The sector inevitably has a high risk/high reward profile but, possibly in the future, risks will reduce as R&D effort becomes more scientifically targeted, as discussed earlier, and such projects become shorter and less capital intensive.

1.3 Medical Devices

The medical devices sector is much more fragmented than the pharmaceutical one and covers a vast spread of products, ranging from high technology diagnostic equipment to low-tech homecare products, such as walking frames. Instead of selling to clearly defined and highly profitable pharma companies, most medical devices companies are selling to cost-conscious hospitals and HMOs in North America and to government organisations, such as the National Health Service, in Europe. Although healthcare expenditure continues to rise worldwide, investors in this sector should be highly selective since companies are selling to a difficult market in which consistent profitability can often be a problem.

There is a growing use of electronics and other technologies in medical devices, such as instruments. This trend is set to continue and the outputs from instruments will increasingly be fed back through on-line systems.

Medical devices and systems will also increasingly be used as protective measures against liabilities and litigation, which are becoming a major threat and cost to the healthcare industry. Examples are contamination control and sterilisation processes which can prevent or, at least, reduce the incidence of MRSA and other bugs in hospitals.

The impact of an ageing population on Western countries is also very important and opens up the potential for medical devices and equipment to combat the problems of age. Examples are the increasing use of hearing aids and homecare products, with the latter both assisting their users and also reducing the costs of nursing treatment.

Medical devices can be a very fruitful area for investment if care is taken to select the right niches and companies. They tend to offer medium risk/medium reward opportunities but can have considerable business stability, once the companies concerned are established.

1.4 Health Information

Medical devices will increasingly be linked to automated on-line information systems, as mentioned earlier. This will both remove transcription errors from previous manual methods and, at the same time, provide rapid availability of patient information to medical staff. The results of this will be to improve patient monitoring and control, thereby saving nurse and doctor time and costs.

The use of email and the Internet in the healthcare industry will continue to grow and will provide a much greater availability and transmission of information within it. Such developments will, however, have to work within the constraints of keeping patient information confidential.

There will be a similar use and handling of databases to improve the diagnosis of diseases and the improvement of treatments. Subject to the confidentiality issue, this will increasingly be used on an international basis.

E-health publishing systems will continue to grow at the expense of more traditional publishing. It will also help feed and satisfy the rising demand by the public for direct access to health information. This trend to consumerism will increase the public's awareness and knowledge of diseases and their treatment, and will also result in more direct advertising of medical products and services.

As the use of electronic communications and the Internet increases dramatically in the future, the health information sector will become very attractive from an investment standpoint. This will particularly be the case when suppliers to the market have found acceptable ways to charge for their services, and as that market matures commercially.

2   The Technology Market

The technology market has annual revenues in excess of US$1 trillion. The US share of this is estimated at 35% with an annual growth rate of 10.5%, based on figures for the largest sector, information technology.

The market is made up of a number of sectors of which the following are now explored:

- Information Technology
- Telecommunications

- Instrumentation
- Consumer Electronics

2.1   Information Technology

The market for information technology in the US totalled US$316.6 billion in 1997 and is currently growing at a rate of 10.5% compared to 12% in 1996. Growth in Europe has been even more dramatic with companies waking up later to the Year 2000 problem. For example, in the UK the IT sector has seen growth of 20% in the last two years but this is expected to slow down to about 10% next year and beyond.

The main factors fuelling growth in the sector have been the impact of Year 2000 and the work required by companies to prepare for it, preparations for the introduction of the Euro, deregulation in areas such as utilities and amalgamations, particularly among financial institutions, which have often necessitated a review and revision of existing systems. Whilst some of the influences of these items will tail off in the future, there is still strong underlying growth in the sector.

The main ingredients of the sector are services, software and hardware. Services provided by IT companies range from consultancy, overall systems design for a client, selection and supply of software and hardware from outside suppliers, through to the full management or provision of a client's IT facilities. Services are now the fastest growing area of the sector, linked to a major increase in outsourcing.

Software, which has been the lead sub-sector in the past, is still important, particularly in areas such as banking and resource planning. The key to success, usually for a software company, is for it to understand the market needs in a particular niche area and industry and develop advanced software, patented if possible, which can be applied in a practical manner to meet them.

Hardware, which was the original spearhead for the sector, has come down so much in price and size, with the increased power and capabilities of modern chips, that it has become the preserve of large companies which can afford the development and marketing expenditure required. There is a strong move away from large legacy-based machines and systems to PCs linked to client servers, with the consequent increase and decentralisation of computer power.

From an investment standpoint, services companies offer a relatively safe and low risk entry since they need little capital in order to get off the ground. However, their growth is often constrained by having to expand their resources to meet increased demand which also can become a difficult management problem, particularly where it exists on an international scale. Many services companies seek to find products which they can exploit behind their services but usually have limited success in achieving their aim, as the cultures and commercial methods of the two are somewhat different.

Software businesses, which often start as consultancies, also offer a relatively safe entry point for an investor for the same reasons. If they are able to develop standard software, which has leadership in their market, they often have good upside but tend to have more volatility and less stability than a services business, since their progress is dependent upon making some major sales of their product and on maintaining their R&D leadership, usually against tough competition.

Hardware does not offer many opportunities for a venture capital investor since the sector is very capital intensive with relatively short product lives. Sometimes opportunities present themselves in the provision of components for computer hardware and these can be interesting, although definitely at the high risk/high reward end of the spectrum.

Probably the most interesting investment opportunities in the sector in the future will be in services, linked to outsourcing, which can produce a range of large industrial and commercial clients prepared to sub-contract their requirements out to an IT services company. Such a movement provides an attractive mix of revenue growth, profitability and cash flow, coupled to large order backlogs. This is similar to the opportunities available to CROs in the healthcare sector, discussed earlier, and can provide a combination of revenue stability and profit growth, through a complementary mix of services and products.

2.2 Telecommunications

Telecoms has been a major growth market for a number of years, due to advances in technology, deregulation, privatisation and globalisation. Whilst growth has been strong, market penetration for mobile phones is only 2% of the world's population compared to 13% for fixed line penetration and there is, therefore, still scope for massive growth ahead.

Fixed line communications have also grown dramatically due to the Internet and the desires within the companies to link their operations internally and to outside customers and suppliers. The real take-off that is occurring, and will continue to occur, is the connectivity between a company's computers and communications systems which gives it tremendous on-line power and advantage in dealing with its problems and customers' needs.

Satellite communications are another thread which can overcome some of the constraints of fixed line communications and open up rural and global opportunities. The full potential and impact of this will be seen in the years ahead.

From a venture capital investment standpoint, mobile phones are too fast-moving and capital intensive from a supplier standpoint to be attractive, although sometimes companies that provide specialist components to mobile telephone companies can offer opportunities. More interesting are communications service companies which are able to harness the technology available to a specific market need, often involving the Internet, and also able to find a way to make money out of the transaction. Many such internet based companies are vulnerable at the moment but will become stronger as the market matures and is prepared to pay properly for the services it uses. The healthcare industry offers major scope for communications and IT companies in the future, although it has been slow to take up the technologies offered to date, such as the use of call centres linking an organisation's telephone and computer systems. Finally, video-conferencing suppliers can be interesting with the growth of that technology due to the costs and frustrations of air travel.

2.3 Instrumentation

There is an increasing application of video and audio technologies within the instrumentation sector and instruments will continue to become more sophisticated, with direct linkage into communication and online systems. This will, as with medical devices and health information systems, eliminate manual transcription errors and provide control information much more quickly.

Instruments will continue to combine different technologies with beneficial results to suit particular applications. Their uniqueness will be in the successful combination of such technologies rather than the technologies themselves which are, in the main, already well-established.

Success in the instrumentation sector for small companies will be achieved by looking for niches in the market which provide them with some protection. The defence industry is such an example since, rather like the healthcare one, it provides good stability and protection.

Instrumentation suppliers will tend to concentrate on the design and marketing of their products in order to keep their costs and exposure down. They will continue to off-load distribution to large companies in overseas markets and will normally sub-contract manufacturing to low-cost areas such as Asia.

From an investment standpoint, instrument companies can offer low risk/medium reward opportunities with a good degree of stability. Those which involve very high cost items are, however, to be dealt with warily.

2.4 Consumer Electronics

This sector is fast-moving and is subject to the vagaries of consumers, where fashions and buying tastes can change quickly. It is, therefore, difficult to find niches which are protected from such trends and from the competitive pressures of large companies.

The sector has good growth but is a dangerous one for a company with limited resources. It also has a wide spread of markets and applications.

With the dominance of large companies in the sector, a small company will be wise to pick its area of activity carefully and concentrate on the quality and control of its products and IPR. Even more so than in instrumentation, it will need to off-load distribution to large companies and manufacture to low-cost areas.

Venture capital investment will clearly be targeted at the smaller niche companies and sometimes at their component suppliers. Even then, the sector tends to offer high risk/high reward opportunities, due to the fast-moving and changing nature of the market.

COMPANY BOARDS: THEIR ROLE AND STRUCTURE

A. Introduction

In recent years there has been a significant change of emphasis in the function of Boards, both in the UK and in the Western hemisphere generally. Some writers such as Drucker have argued that the role of the Board has been superseded by that of executive management; others that the changing social conditions and motives of business call for a stronger, better balanced and more independent Board.

Naturally there are many different views, from a political and sociological standpoint, on the functions and responsibilities which a Board should exercise. One fact, independent of views is, however, clear: the organisation and operations of Boards have not kept pace with their changing roles. The main reason for this is the scant amount of research and analytical study which have been applied to Boards, in direct contrast to the considerable attention which has been devoted to executive management.

This paper seeks in a small way to redress this balance. It sets out some of the problems which face Boards and outlines recommendations for making them more effective. Inevitably, the discussion has to be fairly general because of the breadth of the subject and the variety of situations within it. The views expressed are, as far as possible, independent of political bias, and are based on the principle of achieving maximum effectiveness within the legal and social framework. It is not the author's role to lay down general social doctrines and policies for Boards, but rather to anticipate changes and to seek to adapt solutions to meet individual, and often differing, circumstances.

The paper, in layout, deals initially with the Board's role, past, present and future, within the general economic environment. It then discusses, within the developing role anticipated for Boards, their organisational needs for effective operations, the approach taken being the classical one of discussing in turn:

- Objectives
- Organisational Structure and Staffing
- Supporting Planning and Control Systems

The paper ends with a Summary of Conclusions for improving Boards, followed by a supporting Annex to the paper.

Whilst the paper deals specifically with the British commercial company, for clarity and concentration of effort, the principles of control expounded are applicable on a wider basis. They apply in the main both to non-profit making concerns and to enterprises in other countries.

B. Evolution of Board's Present Role

The limited company was an invention of the mid nineteenth century. At that time, and subsequently, the ownership and management of companies were synonymous and were carried out by the same people. This system was perpetuated for many years through family inheritance of control and worked fairly well, after initial abuses, in the paternalistic environment which then prevailed. Another feature of the time was that businesses were nearly all very small by modern standards.

In the twentieth century and particularly in its last decade many changes have, however, taken place. First, the impact of taxation has made it increasingly difficult for family owned concerns to continue independently. Secondly, the growing size and complexity of business, imposed by technology and competitive conditions, have placed great stress on management capability. In short, many owners of companies have found that they have neither the funds nor the skills to cope with modern conditions. As a result, they have been forced to obtain outside help, both through the stock market to obtain finance and through recruitment of outside managers to increase their expertise.

A gap therefore opened up between owner and manager. Initially this did not create particular problems because in general the managers were appointed by the owners and, in the main, ran the company in the latter's best interests. It was normally accepted that a company should be run to achieve the maximum return on investment to shareholders. As the gap widened, however, and the shareholders became increasingly remote, the power passed into the hands of the managers, who in some cases put their own interests above those of the shareholders.

The situation now prevails, or at least is beginning to prevail, where power is back in the hands of a few people again, but in this case it is the managers rather than the owners. This trend is being accelerated by the recent and continuing spate of mergers and takeovers.

Another factor, which has a direct bearing on the Board's role, is the move towards socialism in most Western countries; this challenges the traditional concepts of the ownership of profits and the way in which a company's surpluses should be distributed. No longer are profits and surpluses universally considered to be the sole prerogative of shareholders.

Finally, there is a strong movement in society away from authoritarianism and in particular a reaction against institutions. Two outstanding examples of this are the Churches and Parliament itself, both of which have been slow to adapt to the times. Society is also becoming critical of business, and particularly of big business. Unless the structures through which business is controlled, namely the Boards, are seen to be efficient and to act responsibly, pressures to introduce drastic changes, both in methods of control and the free enterprise system as a whole, could result. This would be unfortunate because the present arrangements are basically sound, and with adaptation could meet the new demands placed on them.

C. Future Development of Board's Role

Before examining the way in which the Board's role is likely to develop in the future, it is necessary to look more closely at the current industrial scene in the UK. This review, in conjunction with the previous section dealing with past trends, should provide sufficient data for immediate and future needs to be understood.

One of the features of the present situation in Britain is the increasing government and public concern over the way in which power is exercised. There has always been, and will always be, scope for misuse of power but clearly the larger the concentration of power, with the increasing size of industrial and commercial units, the greater the scope for misuse. There have been many examples recently, particularly in the takeover field, of power apparently being applied by directors for personal ends rather than for the good of the enterprise they represent.

The merger movement, initially encouraged by government, has also created problems. The original concept was that larger concentrations of units in similar or complementary industries would enhance the country's international competitive power. In the event, many mergers have not followed this pattern and instead have led to the formation of large conglomerates, some of which would not appear to be in the national interest.

In the face of this situation, retaliatory action is being taken or planned by the different interests involved in commerce. The government, representing the community, has brought pressure to bear directly through nationalisation, and indirectly by seeking to strengthen the powers of central bodies, such as the Takeover Panel; it is also likely to introduce new and wider legislative controls than currently exist. Shareholders, through the media of investment and unit trust, are concentrating their power and are likely to reassert some of their previous influence. Employees, through the unions and often independently of them, are making their case forcibly and demanding an increasing share of potential profits.

The present situation is therefore already a difficult one, and will become increasingly sensitive unless corrective action is taken. The solution to the problem would appear to be to recognise and protect the separate interests mentioned, but to do so in a manner which contributes to the success of the company concerned.

If the company's interests are looked upon as the first priority, then clearly its managers must have sufficient freedom within which to operate to achieve commercial success. Equally clearly, the needs of the different and separate interests involved in the company, including the company itself, must be reasonably satisfied if long-term success is to be assured. The ultimate aim, albeit an ideal one, should be to seek to generate the maximum potential surpluses and then to distribute them in the manner most likely to preserve the company's interests, consistent with a degree of equity.

In fact, the Board has a role in the modern industrial society, but a very different one from that of its nineteenth century ancestor, who it still too closely resembles. Its new role, while still preserving as its main aim the need to run companies efficiently and viably, is likely to involve more definitive social obligations to protect the interests, in different degrees, of all parties concerned in its operations, namely shareholders, employees, customers and the State.

The problems arising from the situation depicted above, have already been recognised on a limited scale. Different countries have evolved different solutions geared to their legal systems and national characteristics, but none of these solutions have been totally satisfactory. In Germany, for instance, the two tier Board system has been in operation for some time and is compulsory by law for public companies. In this arrangement, a supervisory Board is appointed in addition to the more normal management Board. The supervisory Board is responsible for monitoring the affairs of the company from a public accountability point of view and is also responsible for appointing the management Board, though officially it has no management responsibilities of its own. At least one third of the supervisory Board has to be composed of employee representatives; in coal and steel the ratio is a high as 50%. The success of the German economy must at least indicate that this approach to Board control is a tenable one. However, there are disadvantages, and the two tier system has to some extent restricted the freedom of the managers; in particular it has acted as a severe brake on any redundancy plans and has therefore inhibited the mobility of labour. This is of particular relevance to the UK, where mobility of labour is very necessary at the present time.

In Britain, some of the political parties have developed plans concerning the control of industry and these involve changes in legislation. The Labour Party seeks to extend public ownership, either directly or indirectly, and hence, theoretically at any rate, is putting the interest of the nation first. The Liberal Party talks of worker participation in control, and seems to be moving towards German and Dutch practice of worker representation on Boards.

The solutions outlined are all based on the principle of interested parties being represented at Board level in order to enable them to influence or even dictate policy and decisions. This approach ensures that due attention is given to the preservation of individual interests and therefore meets what might be called the trusteeship responsibilities of the Board; however, it has two flaws from a management point of view – 'management' in this sense being defined as the assistance which the Board gives, both directly and indirectly, in the commercial guidance of the company. First, it does not encourage the use of high calibre personnel as Board members, since the role of such members tends to be narrow and sectional, and secondly, it sets the scene for a battle of conflicting interests in the Board room. Both of these features adversely affect Board performance.

A better approach, from a management, but not necessarily a trusteeship point of view, is to treat the Board as a corporate body above the prejudices and biases of any particular sector of the community and to give it the powers to look after all the interests concerned. This can only be achieved if the Board is able to act corporately in a responsible and efficient manager in the interests of society. This pre-supposes that some, if not all, members of the Board have a high level of integrity and performance.

In many concerns there is a strong case, economically at any rate, for executive management to be well represented at Board level. Indeed a survey carried out in the United States indicated that executive Boards produced better results, from a financial

151

standpoint, than their non-executive counterparts. However, a fully controlled executive Board is not well placed to act objectively and operate fully in society's interests. There is, in fact, the need to have society's interests represented on the Board, not individually, but as a whole. This can best be achieved by the use of part-time non-executive directors, who can apply the necessary checks and balances to their executive colleagues. If these 'non-executive' directors are professionally competent and trained for their role, they can carry it out in a positive sense and can make a real contribution to the companies they represent.

In the UK it is unlikely that either of the two basic approaches to Board control specified, namely the two tier system on the one hand and the use of the professional director on the other, will have more than partial application in the foreseeable future. As with most British solutions, a compromise is likely to emerge and different methods of control will probably, and to some extent already do, co-exist side by side in the economy. This is likely to take the following form:

(a) The two tier system for very large companies which affect the national interest, and which are sensitive from an employee point of view

(b) The use of the 'professional' part-time director in many large and medium-sized public companies

(c) The traditional and existing system of family ownership in small private companies, and in larger public companies which have retained control and influence indirectly through trusts etc. Clearly, this pattern of ownership is, and will always be, very important in a private enterprise system.

For the sake of precision and clarity, the rest of this paper develops the approach to Board structure specified in category (b), namely the one based on the use of the professional part-time director. This is mainly because it is considered to have the greatest commercial possibilities for sizeable companies; indeed, even if the concept of a Board having social or trusteeship responsibilities is unacceptable, or irrelevant in certain circumstances, a strong case can still be made out for the professional part-time director in his own right, from a purely managerial standpoint.

A further reason for developing category (b) only is that it is the most comprehensive in concept. Inevitably, therefore, discussion of it will more than cover the ground for categories (a) and (c), and parallels should easily be able to be drawn as required in the discussions that follow.

Finally, the paper does not seek to cover in detail, even for category (b), all the variables which affect Board structure in different industries and companies. For convenience, however, a list of some of these variables and their effects are contained in the Annex at the end of the paper.

D. Objectives and Corporate Activities of a Board

The legal definition of a Board's function, contained in the Companies' Act, can be summarised as 'the business of a Company shall be managed by its directors but the directors may appoint a managing director'. This definition is narrow in one sense in that it does not adequately describe what is expected of a Board, but wide in another in that it allows considerable scope for interpretation. Certainly the definition no longer suffices to cover current UK practise.

It is therefore necessary to specify clearly the Board's function from a more detailed and realistic point of view. The stages to this are first, to look at the basic purposes of a company, then to identify, or at least restate, the Board's role in relation to them, and finally to specify the main activities a Board needs to carry out in order to fulfil its role.

The basic purposes of a business are normally considered to be to supply goods and services, to provide employment and to recompense shareholders. These purposes have moral, social and financial implications to many sectors of society, namely shareholders, employees, customers, creditors, the community (in whole or part), and the State. In this, the Board has, as mentioned earlier, responsibilities of trusteeship as well as of management, and, one of its most important roles is to decide the distribution of funds available between the conflicting priorities of the different groups. There can be no standards for this, but current practise in several well-known companies is to distribute 50–70% of potential surpluses to shareholders, either through dividend distributions or transfers to reserves. A vital point is that, although a Board has responsibilities to many groups, its responsibility to the company comes first, and is overriding.

In the light of its constraints as trustee, the Board's approach to management, either directly or through supervision, should be to seek to achieve the maximum surplus for the company on a continuing basis. Indeed one way in which the directors can properly exercise their role is to consider the company as a real estate and to seek to achieve its continuance in a properly maintained manner over a long period of time.

Inevitably individual Boards will necessarily have to or wish to modify this philosophy to suit differing circumstances, as discussed earlier. They may put the interests of one particular sector of the community much higher than the others, but in a developed country such as the UK, if they tip the balance too far the other sectors will resent exploitation, and will bring pressures to bear to rectify it. The Board's position of trust should not in fact be misused.

To exercise its role properly the Board needs to carry out certain corporate activities. These relate to the key control areas of the company and normally include:

- determining objectives for the company
- approving major strategies
- approving the company organisation
- appointing the top strata of executives
- setting top management compensation
- determining the planning and control systems required to support the organisation, including the information required by the Board to enable it to exercise its role
- approving company plans, both long-range and short-range
- reviewing progress against plans
- approving major company decisions
- dealing with acquisitions, dispositions and mergers, and other matters affecting shareholders
- handling major ad hoc crises threatening the company.

These objectives, strategies and plans will need to be expressed in terms of policies covering such items as new products, marketing, pricing, capital requirement, cash utilisation, personnel remuneration and development, and relationships with outside bodies.

The usual procedure for these activities and policies will be for proposals to be submitted to the Board by the executives, together with all relevant information, and for the Board to exercise the right of approval or amendment.

E. Board Organisation

The use of a corporate body of people to run a company, or indeed any other form of activity, has many disadvantages of which the main are delay in decision making, amount of time wasted in discussion, tendency towards compromises, and of course expense. In many respects a single person can exercise these functions more efficiently and economically. However, with one person there is a concentration of power, with all its dangers, and the tendency for judgements to be more narrowly based and hence less sound. In view of the trustee functions involved in company control and of the need to protect different interests, there is little doubt that a corporate Board is the most satisfactory instrument of control which has yet been devised.

The problem, therefore, is not whether or not a Board is the right instrument, but how it should be organised and run. There is great scope for improvement in current practise in this field.

Types of Board
There are many different types of Board in existence, of which the following are the most typical:

1. *Executive Boards*: composed of full-time executives only. The danger here is similar to that with one man in charge, namely concentration of power with a small group with biased interests.

155

2. *Non-Executive Boards*: composed of part-time non-executive directors. These Boards are fairly common in the banking and insurance world but are usually too detached from the management process.

3. *Mixed Boards*: composed partly of executives and partly of non-executives.

Mention has already been made of one type of non-executive Board and mixed Board, namely the two-tier supervisory Board on the one hand and the Board including the professional director on the other.

Each of the three types of Board (i.e. executive, non-executive, mixed) has worked well in particular circumstances, but the first two are not really suitable as a general solution for the reasons stated. The last type of Board, namely a mixed board, has much to recommend it, particularly when the non-executive directors are professionally competent. It is increasingly finding favour both in this country and in America since it provides a basis for reconciling the trustees and management aspects of a Board's operations. In view of this most of the proposals which follow will relate to mixed Boards, as mentioned earlier.

Whatever type of Board is adopted, however, it is essential that the difference between its role and that of executive management is clearly appreciated; the one is a governing body responsible for guiding and monitoring the overall progress of a company, the other is an executive instrument responsible for achieving success under such guidance. This is plainly stated by the old adage 'directors should direct, managers manage'.

Composition of Boards

The composition of a Board is of vital importance since the balance of skill, experience and objectivity within it will determine its success. First and foremost, is the question of size and the relative representation of executive and non-executive directors. A good deal of research in America has been carried out on this subject and it is generally considered there that Boards should have between five and sixteen directors, of which about one third should be non-executive. Several writers consider a Board of eight or nine as the ideal.

156

Boards with less than five people are unlikely to have sufficient balance of interest, and Boards larger than sixteen are likely to be unwieldy. As *The Economist* put it 'a board of ten is a directorial board and a board of twenty is a debating society'.

Within the overall limits specified, certain other factors need to be considered. These are:

1 SKILLS

The members of the Board should be chosen to provide a balance of skills though it must be remembered that they are acting primarily as generalist members of a corporate body. In particular, non-executive directors, of the professional part-time category, can bring specialist skills to the company, provided they are carefully selected.

2 AGE

There should be representation of different generations on a Board in order to ensure that it is in touch with modern ideas, and also to provide for stability and continuity. Ideally at least one of the Board's members should be in the age groups 35 to 45 years, 45 to 55 years and 55 to 65 years. The modern ideas normally, but not always, come from the younger men/women.

Committees

Committees, sub-committees and subsidiary Boards are specially constructed units to which the Board has delegated particular powers.

The main reason for committees is to undertake an investigation or activity in depth without involving the whole Board in the process. Typical examples are finance committees, executive committees, audit committees, and special committees to deal with one-off projects.

The main emphasis on committee organisation is that the specialist skills required should be fully represented, and that well documented reports should be submitted to the main Board. Sometimes committees are given fully delegated powers to operate on particular matters and where this occurs it is vital that there be main Board representation if the matter is important.

At other times, special committees are formed to deal with matters which affect individual Board members' interests. For instance, committees are often formed of non-executive directors to decide the policy for the remuneration of their executive colleagues. This is another illustration of the importance of non-executive representation on the Board.

F. Individual Responsibilities and Relationships

Having ascertained the corporate role of a Board and its organisational framework, it is necessary to study in some detail the responsibilities of individual members of the Board and the relationships between them.

Director
The first major classification is by type of director and the main categories are dealt with below:

1 EXECUTIVE DIRECTOR
   Executive representation on a Board strengthens its involvement in and rapprochement with management, as mentioned earlier. The executive director must, however, clearly differentiate between his separate roles as executive and director. In the former he is acting as a manager with delegated responsibilities for a particular function; as the latter he is a corporate member of a group and is not representing his particular executive responsibilities. Many executive directors find it difficult to differentiate between their two roles and tend to defend their own actions and interests at Board meetings.

2 PROFESSIONAL PART-TIME DIRECTOR
   The arguments for professional part-time directors, as previously outlined, can be summarised in more detail, as shown below:

   • they are a balancing element on the Board, and can arbitrate in executive conflicts
   • they can act objectively as critics and advisers

- they are able to take a long-term view and hence help future plans
- they can inject specialist skills into the Board if they are carefully selected.

The professional part-time director does not have the same conflict of interest as the executive director. However, he/she does have a special onus to ensure that power is not being misused by the executives, and in order to carry out his duties effectively he must give a good deal of time to his duties; not only at Board meetings, but in between, studying facts and undertaking special investigations as required. As a very minimum the professional part-time director should give one day per month to the company, and often far more.

There is a school of thought that the professional part-time director should not be deeply involved in Board activity since such involvement will impair his objectivity. This school of thought is contrary to the philosophy that a professional part-time director has a real contribution to make to Board activity; it should be rejected, unless special circumstances make it necessary.

3 NOMINAL DIRECTORS

The title 'director' is a very loosely applied one, and many members of companies are nominally called directors, without having any directorial responsibilities. Nominal directorships are normally given to enhance status, and should not be encouraged.

4 LOCAL, SPECIAL OR ALTERNATIVE DIRECTORS

These forms of director exist in certain companies but are not relevant to the main argument and will not therefore be pursued further.

The next step is to examine in even more detail the particular functionaries of a Board, namely the Chairman, the Managing Director and the Secretary.

Chairman

It has been rightly said that the 'effectiveness of any group will never be greater than the skill of the chairman', and a Board is no exception. The Chairman's role is a vital one, and he has particular responsibilities for ensuring that the Board always operates effectively.

The reasons for having a Chairman are usually:

- to chair meetings of the Board (as stated)
- to lead the Board by ensuring positive and imaginative pursuit of the Board's objectives
- to comply with the organisational requirements of the Companies' Act
- to provide management continuity
- to divide the top executive work load
- to provide an honorary position
- to provide a stabilising force.

It is customary for the Chairman to have jurisdiction over finance, legal matters, public relations, stockholders relations, and sometimes corporate planning. His detailed duties in running the board include:

- preparation of agenda
- seeing that proposals have been thoroughly explored
- submitting proposals, and all relevant information, to Board members in advance of Board meetings
- integrating committee discussion and summarising agreements reached
- handling difficult Board members and touchy and contentious issues.

To do his job effectively the Chairman must be closely in touch with his fellow directors and the executives, and must also have a good grasp of all relevant information relating to Board propositions and matters.

If the Chairman is called in to arbitrate on a matter, he must decide if it is (a) a management matter, or (b) a Board matter, or (c) act himself, if urgent, and report to the Board afterwards.

The Chairman's job is in fact in many ways the most difficult and important one in the company.

Managing Director

The Managing Director is the member of the Board to whom the directors, acting corporately, have delegated their day-to-day powers of management. The extent of the delegation will naturally vary to suit circumstances but the need for it is obvious. Just as a corporate body is best placed to guide and govern, so an individual person is the best mechanism for day-to-day administration and control.

The Managing Director has the same dual responsibilities as any fellow executive director, but in addition has the specific responsibility for implementing the Board's policy which he has helped to formulate.

It goes without saying that he must be an efficient administrator but in particular, he must be able to brief his executives clearly on Board policy and aims, and must delegate powers widely to them. Otherwise, the Managing Director's responsibilities are similar to those of any other Board member.

Secretary

The Secretary is one of the two officials specified by the Companies' Act, the other being the Chairman.

The Secretary need not be a director, though he often is. His usual role is to handle administrative matters, such as minutes at Board meetings and also all detailed matters relating to shareholders and the company's official title.

The Secretary of the Board is often the Secretary of the company, and as such, also deals with detailed legal and accounting matters. The two roles are, however, separate and should not be confused.

Critical Relationships

Probably the most critical relationship in a company is that between the Board and the Managing Director (assuming he is the Chief Executive). For this to be effective:

161

- the Board must understand the Managing Director's role
- the Board must establish goals for the Managing Director
- the Managing Director must have the right to obtain the requisite assistance from the Board to achieve the desired goals.

If the relationship is clearly defined and properly operated, the Board can be of considerable assistance to the Managing Director and vice-versa.

Other critical relationships are:

- the Chairman to the Managing Director
- the Board to senior management
- executive directors to Managing Director.

The Chairman and Managing Director are sometimes the same person, and, although this works well in some instances, there is a danger of too much concentration of power and it is difficult for the incumbent to separate his two roles effectively. Where the positions are combined, the professional part-time director has an even more important role to play since (a) he must be even more vigilant to protect the company's interests and (b) he must be able to offer advice to the Chairman/Managing Director who will have no one else to converse with on an equal footing.

G. Staffing, Remuneration and Training

Much has been done recently to encourage recruitment of graduates into industry, to improve management training through the business schools, and generally to place a great deal of emphasis on obtaining first-class managers in industry and commerce. Indeed, both major political parties are committed to reducing taxation on high earned incomes in order to stimulate executive efforts and attract and retain the best talent.

The emergence of trained professional managers should, of course, help to make Boards more effective in the future, since some of the trainee managers will in due course become executive directors and will be more capable of understanding their dual role of executive and director than their predecessors. This development will, however, not in itself cure the problem since it does not answer the question of how professional part-time directors are to be recruited, assuming their need is in due course recognised.

Unless steps are taken, in fact, there is likely to be a shortage of personnel who have the capability and willingness to act as professional part-time directors in the positive manner specified earlier. The steps required are:

1 To increase the current emoluments for professional part-time directors which are too low – partly in order to attract the right calibre of person, and partly in recognition of the considerable amount of time they need to spend in order to do their job properly.
2 To encourage executive directors to act as professional part-time directors of other companies. Many of them would welcome the opportunity of undertaking a semi-social responsibility of this kind and if the idea spread it would provide a very large source of suitable personnel. For such an idea to work, however, there would have to be a sub-stantial change in the attitude of companies to their executives acting in this way. A recent survey showed that only 16% of companies actively encouraged their employees to take on outside directorships.
3 To use specialist careers, such as accountancy, merchant banking and consultancy, as sources of recruitment for non-executive directorships. In fact, to encourage the emergence of a professional corps of non-executive directors and to see this eventually as a career in itself.

In due course it is envisaged that professional part-time directors would be appointed to companies in the same way as any other position, namely through contact, by advertisement or through a selection agency. In these appointments it is vital that considerable emphasis be placed on integrity, experience, knowledge, and capability.

Other steps which should be taken to ensure that Board members are of the highest calibre and fitness are:

- legislation to make Board members offer their resignation at the age of 65 years; there must, of course, be scope for extended contracts by mutual consent
- the provision of training facilities for directors, both executive and non-executive, in order to make them fully understand their directorial responsibilities.

H. Operating Framework

The operating framework of a Board is based upon meetings held. These may be full Board meetings reviewing the company's overall objectives, supported by progress or sub-committees to discuss particular projects.

If these meetings are to be successful and if the Board is to operate efficiently, these meetings must be carefully planned. The main items pertinent to this are discussed below.

Definition of Purpose
The purpose and scope of the meeting, committee or sub-committee should be clearly defined, as should the limits of its authority and the extent to which it can delegate.

Frequency
The frequency of the Board meetings must be geared to the degree of control and will depend to a large extent on the size of the company. The general rule is that the larger the company the more frequently the Board has to meet, though of course other variables, such as the complexity of the business, will affect the issue. A general guide, relating to turnover, is as follows:

- under £1 million, annual or six-monthly meetings
- £1 to £3 million, quarterly, with periodic special meetings
- £3 to £10 million, monthly
- £10 to £100 million, monthly Board and special Interim Committees
- in very large companies, extensive Board activity with wide delegation to sub-committees etc. For instance, Du

Pont has a central policy-making Board of ten full-time members, who have no executive responsibilities at all.

Board meetings should normally be held in the morning and should be limited to between two hours and half a day. Occasionally, meetings should be longer, but a whole day is the outside limit.

The number of management and committee meetings will affect the desirable number of Board meetings required, but in substantial companies, ten to twelve Board meetings per year is a working minimum for efficient operation.

Agenda

The agenda for Board meetings is vital and needs to be carefully prepared and researched by the Chairman. All relevant facts relating to the Agenda should have been prepared and circulated well in advance of Board meetings.

It is vital that the staff work relating to Board meetings is carried out properly and in particular that Board members are well briefed beforehand.

Information

The provision of satisfactory information to the Board is essential to its efficient operation and is discussed in more detail in Part I which follows.

I. Information Requirements

Unless a Board has a satisfactory supply of information on which to base decisions it cannot exercise its functions properly. Normally, the information requirements of a Board should relate to the key result areas that it has set for the Managing Director.

Examples are:

1   DETERMINING OBJECTIVES
    Return on net assets for past years for the company and for its competitors. Also details of the growth of net assets.

2   Approval of Policies
Data on the comparative merits of alternative policies and, if possible, some form of financial model on which to evaluate them. Also market forecasts.

3   Approval of Company Organisation
Details of the organisation chart and of the main executive appointments.

4   Selection of Top Management
Details of executive management and their performance. Also a management development plan for the company.

5   Top Management Compensation
Details of current salaries and emoluments, and also, if possible, of comparative market values.

6   Approval of Planning and Control Systems
Details of the planning and control systems and the information they provide.

7   Approval of Major Plans
Long-range and short-range plans expressed in financial and physical terms, broken down probably by product and division.

8   Review of Progress
A feedback of control reports to provide the basic financial, sales and production statistics to show how plans are progressing. Some monthly error in actual figures against targets is permissible, but a cumulative error is not, or at least it should not be greater than 10% of cumulative profit. Monthly figures in addition to cumulative ones are helpful in that they help directors to make decisions at Board meetings and reduce time.

9   Special Action
Ad hoc investigations require special information and should be produced as necessary. They cannot be specified on a standard basis.

J. Summary of Conclusions

The conclusions of this paper can be summarised as follows:

1   There has been only limited study and attention paid to Board operations in the past, and hence the subject has not developed to the extent that executive management has.

2   The role of Boards has changed but their structure and operating methods have not, and need bringing up to date.

3   In future, Boards are likely to be required to exercise, in addition to other traditional managerial responsibilities, a greater degree of accountability for protecting and balancing the interests of the various parties involved in commerce, namely shareholders, employees, consumers and the State. In short, Board responsibilities will contain elements of trusteeship as well as of management.

4   There are two main ways in which the Board's changing role of trusteeship and management can be carried out; on the one hand there is the German system of a two tier Board, and on the other the concept of using professional part-time directors as a balancing influence in a single Board structure. It is anticipated that developments in the UK will involve a combination of the two.

5   Whilst the Board's social responsibilities will increase, its managerial ones will remain vital and can probably be best achieved, in companies of any size, through the medium of a mixed Board, made up of executive and professional part-time directors.

6   The Board needs to carry out specific corporate activities in order to exercise its role and these are normally the key result areas of control for the company.

7   The size of the Board should be between five and sixteen depending on circumstances, and the composition of the Board should be balanced in terms of categories of director, skills and ages.

8 The individual responsibilities of Board members are important, and need to be clearly defined, as do the relationships between members. The Chairman's role is a particularly important one, and needs to be exercised if the Board is to operate effectively.

9 There is likely to be a shortage of professional part-time directors, unless action is taken to open up new sources of supply.

10 The way in which a Board operates, through meetings and the information it receives are vital to its function. In general, all aspects of its operations need to be carefully planned.

Annex

Variants Affecting Board Structure
The main variants which affect Board structure are as follows:

POLITICAL SYSTEM
The political system which exists in a country determines whether its economy is capitalist, state or mixed. This in turn strongly influences the scope of the Board's operations, and the legislation affecting them. At one end of the scale, shareholders' rights are strongly protected, as in the USA; at the other end, shareholders are extinct and control is entirely with the State, as in the communist bloc. There are naturally many different shades of political colour in between the two extremes.

TYPE OF ENTERPRISE
Board criteria vary by types of enterprise. For instance, a non-profit making school would probably require a very different balance of guidance and control to that of a typical industrial company. Whatever the enterprise, however, some sort of Board activity, or its equivalent, is likely to exist and will normally provide scope for analytical study and improvement.

INDUSTRY

The industry in which a company is engaged will normally affect its Board. It is interesting to note, in this respect, that it has been shown that the organisation and committee structure of industrial companies vary substantially for different industries in the UK.

SIZE

Size is an important factor. Its main effect is that it increases the time span over which a Board is controlling operations. Normally the larger the company the further a Board has to look ahead and the more frequently it has to meet.

INDIVIDUAL CIRCUMSTANCES

The individual circumstances of the company or unit concerned will also play a significant part in determining how a Board should operate. Factors such as the extent of family control or influence, the relationship with the local community, and many other variables will all play their part.

Investment Memorandum Formats

This Appendix sets out formats for the Preliminary and Final Investment Memoranda, together with some notes on the due diligence work required to prepare them. The formats provide a disciplined framework for evaluating and recommending investments but need to be intelligently applied and varied to suit particular situations.

The content of the Appendix is, therefore, as follows:

1 **PRELIMINARY INVESTMENT MEMORANDUM FORMAT**

2 **FINAL INVESTMENT MEMORANDUM FORMAT**

3 **DUE DILIGENCE NOTES**

1 PRELIMINARY INVESTMENT MEMORANDUM FORMAT
(Maximum of 3 pages)

NAME OF COMPANY

1. DESCRIPTION OF BUSINESS AND PRODUCTS
   (Up to 5 lines)

2. DESCRIPTION OF MARKET AND COMPETITION
   (Up to 5 lines)

3. OUTLINE STRATEGY
   (Up to 5 lines)

4. CVs OF MANAGEMENT
   Four lines maximum per CV for up to three key executives (normally Chairman, Managing Director and Finance Director)

5. FINANCIAL HISTORY AND PROJECTIONS
   Three to five year history and three to five year projections of sales, pre-tax profits and earnings per share, where appropriate (in a continuous table). Also sales and pre-tax profits year to date against budget, plus the backlog of orders.

6. BALANCE SHEET
   In summary form for three to five years history and three to five years projections including cash, total debt, net current assets and shareholders' funds (excluding goodwill).

7. QUALITATIVE EVALUATION
   (Up to 10 lines)
   • What is unique about the company?
   • Strengths and weaknesses?
   • Market opportunities and threats?
   • Other pros and cons?
   • What is the potential upside and how can it best be exploited?
   • What are the risks and how can they be minimised?

8. PROPOSED INVESTMENT – DESCRIPTION OF DEAL
   (Up to 10 lines)
   - PE ratios – historic and projected
   - P/sales ratios – historic and projected
   - Discounted cash flow analysis
   - Net asset value/market capitalisation at deal price
   - Debt/equity ratio
   - Interest cover – historic and projected
   - Banking arrangements
   - Timing
   - Costs: What costs are involved (i.e. Accountant's Report etc.)?
   - Other

9. PROPOSED EXIT AND INVESTMENT RETURNS WITH ASSUMPTIONS, INCLUDING FUTURE FINANCING

10. RECOMMENDATIONS AND SPLIT BETWEEN FUNDS IN EXACT AMOUNTS PER FUND AND PERCENTAGES OF TOTAL EQUITY PER FUND

2 FINAL INVESTMENT MEMORANDUM FORMAT

1. INTRODUCTION
   - Purpose of Memorandum
   - Content and Sequence
   - Qualifications, if any

2. EXECUTIVE SUMMARY
   - Précis of Subsequent Sections

3. DESCRIPTION OF BUSINESS
   - Background and History
   - Products and Services
   - Deployment of Resources
   - Strengths and Weaknesses

4. MARKET ASSESSMENT
   - Growth Prospects
   - Customer Base and Potential
   - Competition
   - Opportunities and Threats

5. STRATEGY
   - Corporate Strategy
   - Marketing Policy
   - Product and IPR Policy
   - Distribution and Manufacturing Arrangements

6. MANAGEMENT
   - Review of Key Executives
   - Employment Contracts
   - Resource Requirements
   - Expansion Plans

7. FINANCIAL HISTORY AND PROJECTIONS
   - Five-Year Record (ideally audited)
   - Three-Year Turnover and Profit Forecasts (minimum)
   - Cash Flow Projections
   - Balance Sheet Projections

8. ENTRY AND EXIT VALUATIONS
 • Entry Valuation
 • Finance Required
 • Exit Valuation

9. INVESTMENT PROPOSITION
 • Proposed Financing
 • Projected Internal Rate of Return
 • Terms of Deal
 • Main Risks

10. CONCLUSION AND RECOMMENDATION
 • Recommendation to Proceed
 • Split between Funds
 • Timing
 • The Next Steps

Exhibits

I   Product Literature
II   Market Reports
III   Business Plan (if any)
IV   CVs of Management Team
V   Five Year Audited Accounts
VI   Budget and Management Accounts
VII   Monthly Financial Projections
VIII   Backlog Schedules
IX   Key Legal Documents
X   Due Diligence Findings

3   DUE DILIGENCE NOTES

The due diligence process will include gathering information, broadly in reverse order to the memoranda sequences, on the following:

- Financial accounts and performance
- The management team: past records as entrepreneurs, past employment
- The business: operations products/services, business model, financials, strategy
- The technology, patents and know how
- Prospective customers
- The market
- The valuation
- The company: shareholding, structure
- Other investors' interests
- Suppliers, competitors and strategic partners
- Contracts, obligations and legal issues
- Concerns

The due diligence process should normally start with the most general source of information and home in on specific areas and sources of information.

Sources of information include:

- Reports and research
- Market comparables
- News items
- Players in the industry
- Academics or technologies
- Specialists
- Other investors in the industry
- Members in the target customer group
- Original documents
- Named suppliers and partners
- Named customers
- Lawyers and other professionals
- Members of the management team

The more information gathered from trusted third party sources the better. Where information is gathered from uncertain sources and it is critical to the investment decision it should be crosschecked.

Where dealing with third parties care must be taken to maintain the confidentiality of the company. Where the company has provided names of suppliers, customers, partners and references the questions to be posed or the line of questioning should be agreed with the company in advance.

The time taken and the costs incurred in the process are all done at the venture capital firm's risk and are not normally charged to the company. For this reason if any information comes to light that would stop this investment being recommended, the due diligence should cease and once the executive team has agreed that the opportunity cannot be pursued, then the entrepreneur should be informed that an offer will not be forthcoming and the reasons for this should be given.

The output from the due diligence process should be a comprehensive file of findings together with a summary of findings and a recommendation.

The process should be carried out with the concerns of the executive team in mind and as the information comes to light it should be fed back to the executive team.

Examples of Investment Memoranda

This Appendix contains four examples of Investment Memoranda for the companies, set out in Chapter Twenty-Five, with which I have been involved. In line with the general policy throughout this book, the names of the companies, two of which are in healthcare and two in technology, have not been included and they are referred to respectively as Alpha, Beta, Gamma and Delta Limited.

The first example, Alpha, was an early-stage Internet solutions company, for which an Investment Memorandum is included overleaf. The second example, Beta, was also initially an early-stage company in medical communications but grew to become a larger business and is backed up by an Investment Memorandum, written to argue the case for a second-stage round of financing. The other two examples, Gamma and Delta, are both later-stage entities, for which Investment Memoranda are included, with the former being an industrial instrumentation business and the latter a pharmaceuticals services business.

The Investment Memoranda illustrate the forms proposed in the previous Appendix, although they predated the latter and, therefore, contain variances from it in content and layout. The Memoranda do, however, highlight the general approach recommended for evaluating an investment.

Finally, because of space limitation, most of the supporting appendices and exhibits to the Investment Memoranda are excluded, although the contents lists and main texts give an adequate perspective in each case. Clearly, it is not practical to include items such as product brochures in this book.

1 INVESTMENT MEMORANDUM FOR ALPHA LIMITED

An Early-Stage Internet Solutions Company

INTRODUCTION

The opportunity has arisen of an investment of £2.5 million in new shares in Alpha Limited. The company is raising £3.5 million in total, the balance of £1 million being provided by another venture capital firm. The proceeds are entirely for use by the company for working capital purposes and to fund acquisitions. The proposed allocation of the investment between our Funds is covered later in this memorandum.

THE BUSINESS

Alpha was founded in 1995 by its present Chairman and Chief Executive. It is an Internet solutions company developing and implementing Internet and Intranet strategies for clients which, through the use of (electronic) e-commerce, gives them a competitive advantage and boosts internal efficiency. An initial share offering in 1996 raised £467,000 and in January 1998 a second share issue raised £2 million. The use to which these funds have been put is dealt with in the Financial Section. Alpha itself operates in four units and in addition through a proposed acquisition, ABC Limited.

	Function
Business Development Unit	Sales, Accounting, Marketing
Internet Consulting Unit	Strategic Consulting
Client Services Unit	Hosting, Maintenance, Testing/QA
Production Studio	Designing and Building Complex Websites
ABC	Internet and Media Advertising

Historic forms of marketing using mass media are declining and digital marketing is growing quickly. At the same time there are changes in consumer approach allied to increased purchasing power. Alpha's philosophy is to identify what the impact of

178

these changes means to a business and to help a client implement a strategy for change. Alpha is equipped to assist through the whole spectrum from the initial strategic consulting, to the development and implementation of the solution and finally to the driving of traffic through the sites. Alpha looks to long-term relationships with clients with initial consulting fees leading in some cases to the management of the client's entire Internet requirements. Because Alpha can add value to a client's business in a very direct way, through the benefits of e-commerce, it is also exploring equity or joint venture interests with certain clients.

Alpha combines the creativity involved in a conceptual approach to marketing with the technical skills in designing and building websites and then employing advertising skills to drive business through the websites. To be of real value to a company, a website must be an effective instrument for creating revenue.

The accountability for the advertising is through ABC while each business sector is covered through a separate Practice Area. At present there are Practice Areas for Business, Financial Services, Pharmaceuticals, Products, Marketing, Staff (allowing initial recruitment processes to be performed over the Internet) and E-Retail.

Sales to April 1999 were split approximately 40% E-Business, 40% E-Retail and 20% Financial Services but, with the introduction of such areas as Pharmaceuticals and Staff, the sales mix will change.

Alpha has approximately forty customers with the top ten accounting for approximately 70% of sales.

COMPETITION

Management has stated that, although they are aware of a number of companies that are targeting similar markets, they have not been in direct competition on a regular basis. They believe that demand far exceeds supply in this area and that competition will be from three main sources:

IT Companies

Advertising Agencies

Management Consultancies

FINANCIAL

The company has incurred losses since its formation because it has built up its operating base, hired staff and made several small acquisitions. However, a modest profit is forecast for the current year.

PROFIT AND LOSS ACCOUNT

The historic and projected results are:

	Audited 15 months	Audited	Audited	Y/e 31/12 Forecast
	1996	1997	1998	1999
	£ 000	£ 000	£ 000	£ 000
Turnover				
Alpha	186	1136	1092	3294
ABC	-	-	329	2799
	186	1136	1421	6093
Gross Profit				
Alpha	62	442	583	1549
ABC	-	-	118	995
	62	442	701	2544
Overheads				
Alpha	(388)	(780)	(959)	(1420)
ABC	-	-	(110)	(801)
	(388)	(780)	(1069)	(2221)
Operating Profit/(loss)				
Alpha	(326)	(338)	(376)	129
ABC	-	-	8	194
	(326)	(338)	(368)	323

The Group has incurred a loss for the year to date of £257,000 and therefore to achieve the overall profit for the year the forecast requires a sizeable increase in monthly sales for the remainder of the year. However, the order prospects are encouraging and monthly revenues are rising steadily.

The revenue to 31 May and the management's forecast of the remainder of the year are as follows:

Forecast Revenue			*£ 000*
	ytd	*June to Dec.*	*Year*
Alpha	547	2747	3294
ABC	1107	1692	2799
	1654	4439	6093

Conservative Estimate

Turnover	*£ 000*
Alpha	2201
ABC	2799
	5000

Gross Profit	
Alpha 47%	1034
ABC 35%	980
	2014

At this level the result would be approximately breakeven.

BALANCE SHEET

		Alpha		ABC
	31.12.97	*31.12.98*	*30.4.99*	*31.12.98*
Fixed Assets				
Tangible	72	247	254	130
Investments (ABC)	48	1054	1025	-
	120	1301	1279	130
Current Assets				
Stocks/Debtors	195	448	466	441
Cash	118	668	345	33
	313	1116	811	474
Creditors	(309)	(445)	(316)	(389)
Net Current Assets	4	671	495	85
Deferred Consideration	-	(100)	(110)	(55)
Long-Term Liabilities	-	-	-	(73)
Net Assets	124	1872	1674	87

The firm order book for Alpha is relatively small at around £400,000 but outstanding quotes given a probability weighting based on experience amount to £1.4 million and therefore a more prudent projection for 1999 would be for group turnover of £5 million.

USE OF FUNDS SINCE FORMATION

		£ 000
Funds raised:	1996	467
	1998	2000
		2467
Trading losses & Capex		(1748)
Acquisitions ABC	(400)	
	(80)	
	(20)	(500)
Funds available		219

MANAGEMENT
Chairman and Chief Executive
Founded a company previously which became a leading manufacturer of CCTV systems. Subsequently merged this company into a larger group which he became joint MD of, with specific responsibility for its US operations.

Strategy Director
In 1990 President and Founder of media technology company. He has worked on many interactive technology consulting assignments and is considered an expert in the fields of interactive television, entertainment and consumer interactivity.

Director of Business Development
Before joining Alpha, he held European Managing Director posts at two established companies.

Managing Director ABC
Founded ABC in 1988 having trained at a major agency. Went on to lead the development of creative products in a number of agencies.

Financial Controller and Company Secretary
A Chartered Accountant who joined the company after five years with a leading accountancy firm. The Controller will report to a new Finance Director who will be joining the company shortly and whom we will meet shortly.

There are two experienced non-executive directors which will increase to three with our representative.

Alpha has forty-two employees and operates in London and ABC has twenty employees and is based on the South Coast.

DUE DILIGENCE AND EVALUATION OF THE STRATEGY
We have done financial due diligence on the key managers and with a number of customers. In addition the strategy has been tested with senior people who are in a position to give an informed opinion of the concept.

The overall view is of satisfaction with the services provided by Alpha and with their creativity. There was some doubt expressed as to the extent to which clients would move from spending relatively small sums with the company at the stage of buying consultancy time and setting up websites to the management of complete Internet and Intranet systems for much larger sums. There was, however, a feeling that some large organisations will wish to outsource all their Internet requirements, and this was substantiated by calls which we made to our own industry contacts.

It is widely felt that the area of e-commerce is growing very rapidly and that Alpha is well positioned to exploit this.

The team is well qualified to take the company forward although the projected growth will require more technically experienced and creative people in areas where demand for such people exceeds supply.

Financially the company is well controlled and, although historically there has been some optimism in the budgeting of sales, there appears to be close monitoring of the various activities with full and informative management accounts and a record of audited results being very close to those reported internally. We have been issued with a copy of a limited scope report by a leading firm of accountants.

Proposed Investment and Valuation

Initially another private equity firm was proposing to take £2.5 million of the £3.5 million for this fund raising but, in discussion, it agreed to cede half of this to us. As the deal came near to closing this firm, who have little experience of high growth, high technology companies, felt uncomfortable with judging the speed at which Alpha would develop in the evolving Internet market because it still had to prove itself in terms of sales booked against ambitious targets. Their decision was not based on anything more specific, and they have confirmed that their due diligence was otherwise fully satisfactory.

We now therefore have the opportunity of investing £2.5 million at £1 per share against the current price of £1.20 per share. This values the company at a pre-money valuation of £10 million being x 2 current year's projected revenue.

It is proposed that the Funds subscribe in the following proportions:

184

	£	% of equity
Fund A	500,000	3.67
Fund B	1,000,000	7.34
Fund C	1,000,000	7.34
	2,500,000	18.35

There is an option scheme over 10% of the enlarged equity.

Richard Thompson is our nominated Director on the Board. His fee in this role would be £12,000 plus VAT and reasonable expenses, paid to us.

COSTS

In the event that the transaction proceeds to completion, all costs would be borne by Alpha. Should completion not take place for any reason our Funds would meet 50% of the legal and accounting costs commissioned by the other private equity firms whose advisers we are now using.

CONCLUSION AND RECOMMENDATION

Alpha is an early-stage company but already established in the fast growing area of Internet technology particularly as applied to e-commerce. It has an excellent and growing customer base and creative as well as technical skills. It is led by a successful and ambitious entrepreneur and plans to achieve a flotation during 2000. It could then be a target for a larger IT or media company, probably from America.

The entry price although full in UK terms for a company at this stage is low in international terms and the investment would have the prospect of achieving a high return in a relatively short period of time. The risks are those associated with not achieving expected high growth rates but we believe are outweighed by the potential.

2 INVESTMENT MEMORANDUM FOR BETA LIMITED

A Second-Stage Medical Communications Company

CONTENTS LIST
Executive Summary

Investment Memorandum
1 Background
2 Products
3 Competition
4 Financial Record
5 Investment Opportunity
6 Current Year and Financial Projections 1998 – 2001
7 Funding Requirement and Investment Proposal
8 Options
9 Management
10 Conclusion and Recommendation

APPENDICES:
I   Annual Report and Accounts to 31 December 1997
II   1998 Forecast
III   Group Consolidated Cash Flow 1998
IV   New Product Literature

EXECUTIVE SUMMARY
This Investment Memorandum contains a recommendation to one of our Funds (Fund A) to invest £750,000 in Beta Limited to enable it to make a product acquisition and to provide additional working capital to underpin the Group during the next phase of its development leading to a Listing or a Trade Sale.

Beta was formed in 1985 when Richard Thompson led a syndicate of investors including our Funds to purchase the medical publishing and equipment business of another company. Two new executive directors joined the Group at that time, one to run the UK and Continental Europe business and one to run the US one.

The first few years were devoted to transforming the business into an international medical communications group and by 1997 it had established itself in the UK, USA and Holland (serving Continental Europe) with a Group Turnover of £8.9 million and profit before tax of £421,000.

The Group's products, which consist of sponsored journals, franchised publications and publishing products are all funded through the marketing and promotional spend of pharmaceutical companies. The healthcare markets, in the different countries in which Beta operates, are structured differently which leads to products being developed for a specific region but there is some scope for adapting these products and ideas across the boundaries.

The diversity of the Group is a protection against the effect of difficult conditions experienced in any one market but in 1995 trading was difficult in all areas and this was reflected in the results. Beta's UK and European businesses have been growing strongly since then but there has been a sharp downturn in the US.

An opportunity has arisen to diversify further the UK and European portfolio through the acquisition of the European rights to a new product which Beta UK has been marketing under licence since 1997. This product consists of information sheets on a wide range of conditions and diseases delivered free to general practitioners. The cost of acquiring the rights is £225,000.

Including the expected additional contribution from the new product, the financial projections for the next four years are as follows:

				£ 000
	1998	1999	2000	2001
Revenue	9403	13307	15348	18031
Profit before Tax	310	1296	1814	2601

Two of our Funds, A and B, each already have a significant investment in Beta and it is recommended that it is offered to Fund C as an opportunity to invest in a company which not only is very well known to us and in which it is closely involved but also which could achieve a public listing or valuable trade sale within a three year period.

INVESTMENT MEMORANDUM

1   Background

Beta was formed in 1985 when Richard Thompson led a syndicate of investors to purchase the medical publishing and equipment business of another company for £1.2 million. The chief executive of this business joined the newly formed company as Managing Director. In launching Beta the strategy was to use the existing medical publishing business, operating in France and Germany, as a base from which to build an international medical communications group with headquarters in the UK providing publishing products to be distributed to medical practitioners and financed by pharmaceutical company advertising.

In 1987 the French and German publishing and equipment businesses were sold successfully which enabled Beta to return £786,000 of capital to shareholders and to concentrate on its core business. In the same year a level of funding was supplied from internal resources to support the launch of a company in the USA, Beta Inc., to be run by an ex-colleague of the Managing Director.

Beta now has operating companies in the UK, the USA and in Holland. In the last full financial year to 31 December 1997 50% of turnover originated in the UK, 34% in the USA and 16% in Holland.

2   Products

The common theme running throughout Beta's activities is that all products, whether sponsored journals, franchised publications or publishing projects, are funded through the marketing and promotional spend of pharmaceutical companies. The healthcare markets in the different countries in which Beta operates are structured differently which leads to products being developed specific to a particular geographic region although the Group is always exploring ways in which they can be adapted to cross these boundaries and so gain economies of scale and a higher return on publishing ideas.

The table below sets out the product mix in revenue terms, internationally, of the Beta Group followed by a brief description of the principal products.

Year ended 31.12.97
£ 000

	UK	Holland	USA	Total
Journals	3386	106	2250	5742
Projects	1078	316	834	2228
Franchised Journals	-	917	-	917
	4464	1339	3084	8887

UK

The company has a flagship journal in the UK. This journal is produced twice monthly, and is distributed to doctors in general practice. In the year to 31 December 1997 the revenue was £1,207,000 which earned a gross profit of £437,000. It also has developed a range of supporting journals.

Other publishing products included periodic publications linked to the principal journals and the product being acquired, which is described more fully later.

The non-publishing activities of Beta in all territories in which it operates are all marketed under a different name. These activities provide the pharmaceutical industry with pre-marketing and marketing support in the form of consulting, market research, advisory panels, conference planning, monographs and special projects. This is an area where Beta has devoted more resource during the last few years and is one in which higher margins can be earned than in traditional publishing. In 1997 in the UK a gross profit of £702,000 was earned on £1,078,000 of turnover.

HOLLAND

The principal business in Holland, which also serves the Scandinavian market, is the publication of other parties' journals on a franchise basis.

These activities have brought stable and consistent profits to Beta although the margin at approximately 38% is necessarily lower than on own-journal business.

USA

The US company also has developed a flagship journal, which from its launch in 1987 became the leading journal in the field of managed care. The early success of this journal has been a very important ingredient in Beta's profits in the 1990s and in 1997 despite increasing competition in the area still achieved a gross profit of £784,000 on revenues of £1,278,000. More recently there has been a decline in the advertising revenue which is in part due to increased competition but which also reflects structural change in healthcare in the US involving a shift in marketing effort by the pharmaceutical companies from the physician to the consumer. As in the UK, the US company has developed a range of ancillary products.

A new product, the cardbook, has also been developed but despite encouraging support from the pharmaceutical companies, it has not yet earned significant revenues. The cardbook is designed to be carried by members of healthcare organisations and provides members with a guide to their health plans and treatment. The information contained in the cardbook offers pharmaceutical manufacturers an opportunity to inform health plan members, physicians and pharmacists of treatment options when a prescription is written.

3 Competition

In all Beta's product areas and markets, competition is keen. In the journals business in the UK, for example, there are four weekly publications, while in the twice monthly market in which Beta competes there are three significant rivals. There are also eleven journals in the monthly market.

As referred to earlier, a keen competitive environment also operates in the USA.

4   Financial Record

The five year financial record of the group has been as follows:

	1993	1994	1995	1996	£ 000 1997
Revenue	8278	8363	7742	8648	8887
Gross Profit	3548	3921	3513	4029	3888
Gross Profit %	42.9	46.9	45.4	46.6	43.7
Net Profit before Tax	497	756	169	412	421

Beta is sensitive to three geographical markets and each operates independently of the other. The diversification into project work has helped protect the Group from fluctuations in any one market but in 1995 difficult trading conditions were experienced in all markets, due, in particular, to a spate of mergers and restructuring within the pharmaceutical industry and this caused a sharp decline in the overall profits.

Since then the more profitable business of Beta has been brought on but while still absorbing development costs this was not sufficient to counteract the continuing competitive pressure in publishing. The improved but static profit record of 1996 and 1997 disguises varying performances within the Group with continuing depressed revenue from the US but a firmly improving position in the UK. In Continental Europe the performance has remained healthy.

5   Investment Opportunity

Since May 1997 Beta UK has been marketing a product under licence from a company in Australia. This product earned Beta a gross profit in 1997 of £183,000 on revenue of £400,000. It is in the area of patient education which has been identified by Beta as one which has and will experience significant growth. The product consists of attractively packaged, bound collections of tear-out information sheets on a wide range of conditions and diseases. It is delivered free to 12,000 general practitioners in the UK and is updated and issued annually. These sheets are handed to patients as appropriate to their condition and not only provide the patient with a better understanding but also improves compliance with treatment. For the sponsoring pharmaceutical company it provides a unique and uncluttered advertising medium giving continuous exposure within each therapy area for a year. In 1997 sixteen topics were covered.

Beta has identified the new product as a valuable tool in providing information to pharmaceutical companies through patient tracking. A built-in response mechanism will produce a register of patients which will become a market research tool for the industry. Of the new product sheets 45% are given in connection with first-time prescriptions. There is also a trend towards direct to consumer promotion, now legal in the US, which could be followed in the UK. The new product could be an ideal vehicle for this. To secure this business for Beta and the margin which can be earned (50%), an agreement has been negotiated under which Beta acquires the European rights to cardbook for a one-off sum of £225,000.

The projected gross profit which could be earned from the new product over the next two years is shown below. The only additional overhead would be £50,000 pa to cover sales and administration.

		£ 000
	1998	*1999*
UK/Ireland		
To GPs		
Sheets	290	300
Anatomical Flip Chart	30	40
To Pharmacists		
Over the Counter		
Drugs	–	100
To Consultants		
Secondary Care	50	
Direct to Consumer Promotion		
Patient Tracking	–	10
Market Research		
GP Tracking	–	10
	320	510

These figures do not include an expected launch into other European markets. Beta is currently exploring other opportunities in France, Holland, Denmark, Belgium, Italy, Greece and Turkey.

6   *Current Year and Financial Projections 1998–2001 (including cardbook)*

For the six months to 30th June 1998, the result has been as follows:

	Total	UK	Holland	USA	£ 000 Head Office
Revenue	3737	2199	598	940	-
Gross Profit	1740	996	302	442	-
Overheads	(2145)	(1087)	(163)	(865)	(30)
Profit/(loss) before tax	(405)	(91)	139	(423)	(30)

Although the Group is trading behind the original budget, it is normal for a loss to be incurred in the first half of the year. With the poor performance in the USA in part off-set by a better than budget result from the UK and Europe, the projections for 1998 take full account of the position to date.

The projects for 1998 to 2001 have been considered in detail but as regards those for the US, they could be strongly influenced by the level of sales of its newly developed cardbook. This is a new concept for Beta Inc. and would be a volume sale incurring very low overheads. There can be no certainty that significant revenues will be earned from the cardbooks within the timescale of these projections and only a modest level of business has been included.

	1998	1999	2000	£ 000 2001
Revenue				
UK	5545	7304	8875	11035
Holland	1246	2184	2409	2625
US	2612	3819	4064	4371
	9403	13307	15348	18031
Gross Profit				
UK	2722	3661	4678	6175
Holland	567	775	859	938
US	1306	1706	1853	2021
	4595	6142	7390	9134
Profit/(loss) before tax				
UK	487	861	1206	1857
Holland	238	359	399	438
US	(347)	176	319	426
Head Office	(68)	(100)	(110)	(120)
	310	1296	1814	2601

The sensitivity that can be applied to these projections relates in large measure to the performance in the US. With no recovery in the journal advertising business and a disappointing level of cardbook sales, the profit of the Group for 1998 could be in the region of £250,000 and 1999 just in excess of £1 million. Including cardbook sales at the highest end of expectations, the 1999 profit could reach £1.5 million.

Before completion of an investment by the Fund, the Secretary will undertake a review of the projections in the US.

In the light of the recent poor performance in the USA, savings of US$100,000 will be made in 1998 with further more substantial savings in 1999 and 2000. These are taken into account in these projections.

7 Funding Requirement and Investment Proposal

As discussed earlier, Beta is ready to enter into an agreement to acquire the European rights to the new product at a cost of £225,000. It is clear that this could only be financed out of the Group's overdraft facility of £500,000 which is already being drawn on as a result of the poor trading in the US. The Board would not be prepared to use the short-term facility for the purchase of the new product and indeed feel the need for a greater level of comfort in meeting fluctuating cash needs until such time as Beta Inc. is brought back into profit.

These two considerations have lead the Board to agree to seek £750,000 from our new Fund C. The intention is to do this as a private placement, providing existing shareholders approve this approach.

It is proposed that these funds are introduced as equity, in ordinary shares at the same valuation, £8 million, as applied at the last investment by shareholders in 1993. This places a value on Beta of 90% of historic revenue and 85% of projected 1998 revenue. Before the impact of options, an investment of £750,000 would represent 8.55% of the expanded equity.

PRESENT SHAREHOLDERS

		%
Fund A	60,055	38.66
Fund B	25,578	16.46
Other Investor	14,198	9.14
Directors	42,238	27.19
Proposed Issue	13,283	8.55
	155,352	100.00

8 Options

Options are outstanding or are committed over a further 15,735 shares (8.42% of the fully diluted equity following the proposed financing) and consideration is being given to a further small allocation to key executives in the UK within the overall limit of 10% of the expanded equity.

9   Management

The management at other levels has also been strengthened. The Secretary has been appointed to the Group Board as Finance Director and several senior appointments have been made in the projects business where significant growth is targeted.

10   Conclusion and Recommendation

Despite its recent set back in the US, where clear action is being taken to minimise losses while also seeking to build the business, Beta has built a business with revenues in excess of £8.5 million, a strong client base and an excellent reputation in its markets. Achievement of the projections and a uniformly good performance in the three geographic areas in which it operates should make the Group a candidate for a listing during the course of the next three years or alternatively could command a high value in a trade sale.

The institutional investors have been in the company for some time and already have a sizeable investment and therefore it is recommended that they are not pressed to participate in this financing which is offered to Fund C, a newly formed fund directed specifically at companies either near to a listing or already public.

(The Appendices listed in the Contents earlier are not included because of space limitations.)

3 INVESTMENT MEMORANDUM FOR GAMMA LIMITED

A Later-Stage Industrial Instrumentation Company

1   Introduction

We hope that we are drawing close to finalising this transaction. You will remember that a condition of the sale of Gamma Limited is that it should consist of the fibre-optics division only. Therefore, it was agreed that our funds should fund the sale of the non fibre-optics parts of the business as a BIMBO (buy-in management buy-out). This memorandum is mainly concerned with securing your approval to this. You have already given your approval to the sale of the company minus the non fibre-optics division and the Funds have signed an irrevocable letter of undertaking to that effect.

2   Sale of Gamma Limited

In order to put the whole thing in perspective, I will start with setting out the terms of the offer for the fibre-optics division. The acquirer, which is already an important customer of Gamma fibre-optics has formally offered to pay £60m for Gamma Ltd, conditional on the prior disposal of the non fibre-optics parts.

They have offered £21.0386 per Gamma share up front (£57m) plus £1.1166 per Gamma share deferred for a year against warranties (£3m). The effect on our Funds' holding is as follows:

Fund	No of Shares	Cost	Value	Gain
A	547,470	1,477,470	12,129,307	10,651,837
B	372,589	1,027,395	8,254,784	7,227,389

This is the prize that we are looking for and it needs to be remembered in the context of the buy-out, which we would not necessarily have recommended if it had come to us as a stand-alone investment.

3   The Buy-Out Business

You will find attached a business plan prepared initially by us and updated by the buy-in candidate. It is now out-of-date in its detail because there are continuous changes to what we are actually buying.

It is proposed that we buy the shares of the digital meters subsidiary, the business assets and liabilities of the knobs and analogue meters businesses and a number of shell subsidiaries.

The price for these things, as agreed in the offer for sale document from the acquirer is net asset value. You can imagine that we are having a difficult time pinning down what this consists of. The acquirer wants to buy an absolutely clean company, cash and debt free. For £60m, one cannot blame them. This means that the BIMBO vehicle, currently called, after much deliberation, NewCo, (but likely to be renamed Gamma Instruments Ltd), must take the rest (also debt free, cash free). Since Gamma has been in existence for many decades, it has built up a 'history' that is not straightforward. The idea is that NewCo will pay Net Asset Value for these bits, the consideration for which will be used to settle the debts in Gamma Ltd prior to completion of its sale. Any surplus would be paid to the Gamma shareholders by way of dividend. Any deficit would in principle come out of the retention account.

NewCo have employed our auditors to review the net asset position that NewCo would be acquiring and we have their draft report. As at 25 November, the net asset position is £2.6m. We expect that there will be a number of further provisions to be made and the final negotiation takes place this Friday (26th). However, this figure is moving up and down daily.

We have also asked our auditors to review the business plan projections. They have applied some prudent sensitivities which indicate that the peak borrowing position of NewCo might reach £900,000. The unsensitised versions shows peak outflow of about £500,000. We would want to have some headroom above the sensitised version of £500,000 (about two months' expenses). We think that we can get bank borrowing for £1m. However, this has not been formalised. Therefore, the funding requirement is a maximum of £3m.

4   The Proposed Deal

This paragraph replaces para A.2.3 of the business plan. Assuming that the funding requirement is £3m the proposed structure is as follows:

	£	
Institutional Ordinary shares	120,000	for 66.66% of the equity
Buy-In Candidate Ordinary shares	60,000	for 33.33% of the equity
Institutional loan stock	2,820,000	
	3,000,000	

There would be an ordinary share option scheme over 10% of the enlarged equity that would dilute the funds to 60%. There would be a super option scheme over a further 10% of the equity for management super performance. The exercise price in the latter scheme would escalate in such a way so as to give the institutional funds a 30% IRR before the option is worth exercising (only on float or sale).

The loan stock would carry a coupon according to the following table:

Year 1	0.0%
Year 2	5.0%
Year 3	7.5%
Year 4	Libor+2%
Year 5 onwards	Libor+5%

It would be repayable according to the following table:

Year 1	0
Year 2	250,000
Year 3	500,000
Year 4	500,000
Year 5	500,000
Year 6	1,070,000

This schedule has not been matched up to the cash flow forecast because the latter has also been a moveable feast. The idea is that the Funds would have the right to demand payment though, in practice, it would not be sensitive to insist on it if that busted the company. It stops management hanging on to the money or using it for other purposes without our agreement. I do not propose an extra penalty if a repayment is not made on time. It will attract the increased interest rate anyway. However, arrears of dividend should attract a Libor+5% rate.

To the extent that the consideration turns out to be less because of further provisions, it is likely that the cash required in NewCo at the start will be higher by the same amount to pay for those provisions when they crystallise. Therefore, the overall funding requirement will not change. The Funds should be aware of the possible need for further funds down the line.

5   Due Diligence

Our auditors have done extensive work to protect our position. There have been issues in the areas of pensions, group relief, employment law, rates, DTI grants, supply contracts, stock, plant, PAYE, and so on.

Our lawyers are advising NewCo on the legal aspects including employment, pensions, tax etc.

The Gamma pension fund actuary is advising on pension options and possible liabilities.

Another leading firm of accountants have been helping prepare the forecasts.

6   Timetable and Recommendation

The timetable for this deal is being driven by the acquirer who are in the position of 'piper'. They want to have the deal complete bar placing the insurance on the warranties by Tuesday, 30 November. The Gamma shareholders will be insuring the warranties that they are giving on both the Gamma acquirer deal and the Gamma/NewCo deal. There is an absolute deadline of twenty-one days from 20 November. We feel that we can push back a day and allow Fund B to discuss the deal at the meeting next Wednesday.

We recommend that the funds approve this proposal in the

context of the overall pair of transactions. Please give me a ring with any questions you have preferably before we meet so that I have a chance to find out the answer to any awkward one.

BUSINESS PLAN
Gamma Instruments Ltd
November 1999

CONTENTS LIST

A. Introduction and Summary

A.1 INTRODUCTION

The prior disposal of 'residual Gamma' is a pre-condition of the acquirer deal and, therefore, is scheduled for completion on 24th November. Our auditors have been appointed to value the residual Gamma 'balance sheet' as at 15 October, making adjustments to it to cover the period to 24 November. This process is under way.

An MBI candidate, an experienced General Manager with a good instrumentation industry background, has indicated his agreement to join NewCo as Executive Chairman. The management team may be further strengthened by recruiting an experienced General Manager/Operations Director from outside the company.

We aim that the valuation should include all residual assets and liabilities plus taking into account restructuring and non-recurring costs, plus contingent assets and liabilities, plus including provisions for further redundancies which will be inevitable over the next 6–12 months as part of the integration of digital meters into Gamma's operation.

The proposed deal is for our Funds to buy the deal for NAV, so that the larger deal can go through on time, and later, say in early 2000, once the integration process is further advanced, to sell down say 50% of it to other VCs or shareholders. Gamma shareholders will be given the opportunity to invest in NewCo.

A.2 SUMMARY

A.2.1 Aim and Strategic Summary

1) Aim

The aim is to build an electro-mechanical and electronic instruments and components company around Gamma's profitable knobs and meters business with a strong focus on extending the digital meters' sales and distribution networks, and Gamma's customised manufacturing capability. Financial aims are to achieve 10–12% PBT on sales by Year 3 and a cash surplus. Exit aim is to sell Gamma Instruments Ltd to a larger group in three years at a PE in the range 10–12.

2) *Strategic Summary*

Phase 1 is a consolidation phase which will take twelve to eighteen months to complete. The digital meters' costs have been heavily reduced as part of the transfer into the Gamma plant, but the integration of knobs and meters into one company is a challenge on which we have just embarked. A cautious view has been taken of profitability in Year 1 and 2, so as to take a conservative view of cash requirements and to enable the integration to be effectively completed.

Phase 2 is a growth phase (Years 2 and 3) in which we aim to hold the line in meters and knobs, being the 'last and the best'. Digital meters' sale and distribution networks will be fostered, in catalogue, direct sales, selective distributors and large original equipment manufacturers (OEMs), in the UK, Europe and the USA, all current digital meters' markets.

Product development emphasis will initially be an enhancement of existing products and the tightening of specification for high value added top end applications (e.g. waterproofing). Further broadening of the product portfolio through seeking lower cost supply sources will be done. The buy-in candidate will be leading the way forward in this product/market strategy.

Gamma's customised manufacturing prowess will be brought to bear, not only to support the expansion of digital meters but to seek high growth sector electronic components supply alliances with large customers, e.g. in the growing telecoms market through the Gamma fibre-optics relationship. This again will be led by the buy-in candidate.

A.2.2   Financial Projection Summaries

Opening Balance Sheet:
£2.518m

Three-Year Financial Projection Summary

	Year 1	*Year 2*	*£000* *Year 3*
Sales	7,328	7,524	8,512
Gross Profit	3,758	3,915	4,428
Costs	3,768	3,703	3,697
PBIT	(10)	212	831
Interest	51	45	0
PBT	(61)	167	831
NTA	2,457	2,592	3,012

PBT is projected to grow from £61,000 in Year 1 on sales of £7.3m to £831,000 in Year 3 on sales of £8.5m. The full effects of cost savings are projected to come through in Year 2 and 3. Net tangible assets are projected to grow from £2.4m at end Year 1 to £3.0m at end Year 3.

Gearing
A NIL opening overdraft on the pro-forma balance sheet is assumed. This will be confirmed or adjusted in November. Cash is projected as being positive from Year 3 onwards.

A.2.3   Proposed Funding Structure
Using a NAV of £2.518m the funding structure is proposed as follows:

		£000
1.	Ordinary shares: our Funds – 70%	140
2.	Buy-In Candidate – 30%	60
3.	Redeemable Preference Shares (RPS):	2,318
		———
		2,518

The RPS would carry the following dividend coupon:

Year 1	Nil
Year 2	5%
Year 3	7%

A management option scheme of up to 10% of the fully diluted share capital is proposed.

IRRs

Profitable Instrument Groups are currently selling in the range of a 10–12 PE depending on profitability, market sector, potential economies of scale, etc.

PE x 10:	IRR = 30%
PE x 12:	IRR = 35%

A.3   CONCLUSION

We have a strong Manager with a good profit record who knows the instrument and electronic components industry well, who will be devoting much time, first, to integrating the three businesses into one and then to build digital meters and Gamma's manufacturing capabilities and reputation internationally. Provided we can take ruthless action in the short term to cut costs and maintain output, particularly at digital meters, and provided the sales at the meters and knobs businesses hold somewhere close to their current levels, the above strategy should result in a business which could be sold in three to four years' time for a reasonable development capital return.

(The rest of the Business Plan is not included as it merely provides supporting detail to this Summary.)

4 INVESTMENT MEMORANDUM FOR DELTA LIMITED

A Later-Stage Pharmaceutical Services Company

CONTENTS LIST

A   Executive Summary
B   Introduction
C   Product/Service
D   Market and Strategy
E   Competition and Industry Trends
F   Financial Track Record
G   Key Management
H   Deal Structure
I   Board Representation
J   Pros and Cons
K   Conclusion

APPENDICES

I   Due Diligence Summary
II   1996 Business Activities by Type
III   1996 Analysis of Revenue by Client
IV   Competition
V   Key Personnel – CVs
VI   Audited Accounts – year ended 30th November 1996
VII   Group Projections 1997 – 1999

A   Executive Summary

Delta is a medical communications agency which supplies services on a contract basis to the international pharmaceutical industry. The official term used to describe Delta is a Clinical Communication Organisation (CCO).

The opportunity has arisen to invest £3,585,000 through the purchase of existing shares in Delta which it is proposed to allocate as follows:

Fund A	1,185,000	33.05%
Fund B	1,500,000	41.84%
Fund C	900,000	25.11%
	3,585,000	100.00%

This allocation satisfies Fund A's right to participate up to 30% of an investment, allows for Fund B to take a holding of £1.5 million which is a level that we would see as appropriate for this Fund and provides for a smaller investment in the newly launched Fund C.

The increased opportunities for outsourcing in the international pharmaceutical industry, which seeks to flex resources by exchanging fixed costs for variable ones, has led to the growth of the CCO industry. Just as contract research organisations (CROs), became an extension of their clients' drug development capabilities, CCOs are becoming an extension of their marketing teams. A CCO typically provides marketing services from three to five years before the run-up to a drug's launch and may then continue into the post commercialisation phase. Its role is to promote the drug to a carefully targeted audience of physicians and industry opinion leaders, whose understanding and acceptance of the drug is so vital to its commercial success. This is achieved through various media including conference organisation and promotional literature.

The Chairman and Chief Executive of Delta has considerable relevant experience and is well respected within the pharmaceutical industry. He comes across as a man of vision in terms of his strategy for Delta, as well as being sound commercially. His core team have worked together for ten years during which time the company has built up a reputation for quality and consistency.

Net revenue and profit before tax in the year to 30 November 1996 were £12.1m and £1.8m respectively. The £3.6m investment in existing ordinary shares would acquire 11.95% of the company, valuing it at £30m. The rest of the shares would be owned by management. The offer represents a PE of 20 on historic profits and a sales multiple of 2.5 on trailing net revenues, Liquidity would be achieved through the company's flotation on NASDAQ, possibly in two or three years.

We believe that this investment offers an exciting opportunity to participate in an emerging international growth sector, where we can add value through its relevant experience in the field, with Richard Thompson going on the Board.

B   Introduction

Delta is a medical communications agency which supplies services on a contract basis to the international pharmaceutical industry (for due diligence summary, see Appendix I). The official term used to describe Delta is a CCO. The company was incorporated twelve years ago and was originally owned by a US parent. The existing senior management joined the company in 1986 and the CEO led a buy-out in 1990, acquiring 100% of the share capital itself. The CEO and two if his fellow directors are former employees of a major pharmaceutical company.

The company has a staff of 200 operating in the UK on the South Coast and in the US on the East Coast. It has recently acquired a medical communications company, based in New Jersey, and specialising in US domestic medical education programmes, in order to strengthen its US presence.

C   Product/Service

Delta provides strategic marketing services to pharmaceutical companies. This role requires it to interpret, formulate and communicate complex clinical and commercial messages that prime the market prior to regulatory approval of a drug and support and extend brand utility post launch. Specific business activities include conference organisation, scientific writing and editorial services, medical publishing, design and graphics, multimedia and media relations. (See Appendix II for 1996 breakdown).

In the UK, Delta and its subsidiaries offer international marketing services to drug companies with European and North American based headquarters. Its US office, provides both international and domestic marketing services to US companies. Its newly acquired subsidiary holds Continuing Medical Education (CME) accreditation which authorises it to provide training courses for doctors. These courses keep practising doctors up-to-date with current medical knowledge and are largely funded by pharmaceutical companies through arms-lengths grants.

Delta usually takes part in a competitive pitch (based on fixed price contracts) for individual drug programmes, unless it has 'preferred provider' status with a drug company. Once business is secured, it is normal practice for Delta to begin its marketing programme three to five years before launch and this may carry through into the post-marketing phase. The drug company allocates Delta an annual budget for clearly defined activities.

Individual employees at Delta are assigned to look after specific accounts on a long-term basis, in order to develop highly personalised client relationships. Delta's first stage of input is in consultancy work (e.g. accessing market size and client objectives). This is followed by the editorial team's analysis of clinical data (gathered from trials and fed into a database) to gauge if Delta has the right information to market the product. Delta then discusses a programme with the client on how to release information into the purchasing community for optimal effect. In a typical marketing programme, Delta will arrange for the drug to be promoted both at major international conferences and at smaller individual meetings, and will create and distribute literature on the drug.

D   Market and Strategy

The clients of Delta are pharmaceutical companies seeking to raise the awareness of the medical community to drugs in the post-Phase II stage of the trial process and its target market are the physicians and opinion leaders whose understanding and acceptance of new drugs is vital to their commercial success.

Delta currently numbers six out of ten of the top drug companies amongst its clients. Whilst Delta is often dependent upon a single client for a significant portion of its annual revenues (see Appendix III), the risk is lessened by the fact that the overall figure is made up of multiple projects which are run completely independently and are at differing stages of their life cycles.

The CCO industry is evolving in response to the shift to outsourcing by pharmaceutical companies, driven by their need to reduce head-count and lower fixed costs. In order to flex resources, drug companies are drawing on agencies as an extension of their own marketing teams. The rapid growth in outsourcing began in the 1980s and led to the creation of contract research organisations. The CCO industry shares parallels with the early stages of the CRO industry and is said to be five years behind the latter in its development. The currently outsourced CCO industry is estimated at $2–3 billion with an annual market growth rate of 25–30%.

Delta represents less than 1% of this highly fragmented market and is one of the larger CCOs offering international marketing services. The company intends to grow organically but also through a small number of acquisitions, taking advantage of industry consolidation. The company's immediate goal is to make further inroads into the large US domestic market, which has historically remained separate from the international market and been served exclusively by home-grown agencies. Delta has the advantage of close contacts at major US drug companies on the international marketing side, which it can use to leverage itself into the US domestic market. Delta is also favoured by the trend towards greater amalgamation of international and domestic marketing teams. Delta aims to grow its US business to eighty to a hundred people within the next two to three years, and to consolidate both US companies into one building.

E   Competition and Industry Trends

Although competing agencies offer similar types of services, Delta has been successful in developing and nurturing long-standing relationships with clients, and thus maintaining a good quality of earnings. Delta's area of operation is understood to be 'very much a relationship business', where chemistry between individuals in the client company and the agency are all important. Due to the experience gained by its CEO and other staff from working within the pharmaceutical industry internationally, the company has acquired a good understanding of industry issues and has built up useful contacts within it.

The competition comes from a number of UK and US companies (see Appendix IV). No one company dominates the market. Delta offers a more integrated range of services than many of its competitors since it combines consultancy, multimedia and publishing expertise in one company.

While the trend within the CCO industry is towards increasing co-operation and mergers to meet the demands of the pharmaceutical industry environment, it remains highly fragmented. The causes of the trends towards fewer CCOs include:

- Integrated drug programmes requiring both global and localised marketing skills from CCOs.
- The continuing globalisation of the market through technological advances.
- Pharmaceutical companies establishing 'preferred provider' relationships with CCOs.
- CCO specialisation in therapeutic areas and new communication methodologies.

F Financial Track Record

Profit & Loss

Audited Accounts					£000
	Y/e	Y/e	6 mths to	Y/e	Y/e
	May 93	May 94	Nov 94	Nov 95	Nov 96
Turnover (Gross)	7,230	9,332	8,167	16,001	18,875
Cost of Sales	(2,816)	(4,264)	(4,855)	(7,902)	8,764
Gross Profit	4,413	5,067	3,313	8,099	10,111
Operating Profit	667	591	357	1,372	1,604
PBT	755	695	418	1,542	1,828

Consolidated Balance Sheet £000

	30 Nov. 96	30 Nov. 95
Fixed Assets		
Intangible	192	227
Tangible	2,490	2,243
	2,682	2,470
Current Assets		
Stocks	2,491	1,842
Debtors	6,074	2,716
Investments	493	-
Cash	2,700	3,251
	11,758	7,809
Creditors: Amounts Falling due within One Year	(11,666)	(7,682)
Net Current Assets	92	127
Total Assets Less Current Liabilities	2,774	2,597
Deferred Tax	(66)	(252)
	2,708	2,345
Share Capital & Reserves	2,708	2,345

Share capital 1,440 ordinary shares of 5p each to be increased to 1,908 shares following exercise of management options.

Financial Projections are as follows

	1997 Y/e Nov	1998 Y/e Nov	£000 1999 Y/e Nov
Gross Fee Revenue	26,534	33,011	40,684
Net Fee Revenue	16,654	20,797	25,631
Gross Profit	13,690	17,390	21,454
Overheads	(9,752)	(12,081)	(14,310)
Interest	262	290	330
Operating Profit	4,200	5,599	7,474
Pre Tax & Bonus	4,154	5,548	7,414
Profit Share Provision	(750)	(820)	(900)
PBT	3,404	4,728	6,514

G   Key Management (see Appendix V for CVs)

CHAIRMAN AND CEO
He is responsible for corporate strategy and new business generation at Delta.

FINANCE DIRECTOR
He is responsible for financial and secretarial activities at Delta.

EXECUTIVE DIRECTOR
He is responsible for new client development at Delta.

EXECUTIVE DIRECTOR
He now runs the Delta office in Connecticut and is responsible for IT development within Delta.

MD OF DELTA SUBSIDIARY
He runs the graphics and multi-media groups of Delta.

FOUNDER OF DELTA SUBSIDIARIES
Has a background in medical marketing, communication and education and has know the CEO professionally for many years.

H   Deal Structure

Net revenue and profit before tax in the year to 30 November 1996 are £12.1m and £1.8m respectively. The £3,585,000m investment in existing ordinary shares would acquire 11.95% of the company, valuing it at £30 million. This represents a PE of 20 on historic profits and a sales multiple of 2.5 on trailing net revenues, or a prospective PE of 13 and sales multiple of 1.1 on the current year's profits and sales respectively. Liquidity could be achieved through the company's flotation on NASDAQ, in early 1998. On an exit PE of 25 in the year 2000, the IRR on a 10% equity stake could be in the region of 54%.

Post Money Share Structure

Founder	69.50%
Other Directors	18.55%
Our Funds	11.95%

There is an unauthorised share option scheme in operation for 10% of the equity, available to management and other employees with over five years' service. These options may only exercised in the event of flotation. Existing investors would be diluted on a pro rata basis, reducing our Funds' stake to 10.8%. The terms of the option scheme will be reviewed but in no event will total options available for issue exceed 10.0% of the enlarged equity.

I Board Representation
We will have a significant role in the development of the company and especially in its move towards a public listing on NASDAQ through Richard Thompson's place on the Board. The fee will initially be £15,000 pa.

J Pros and Cons
International client base
Growth sector serving the pharmaceutical industry
Provider of integrated services with strong UK/US access
Impressive management with high quality reputation

CONS/RISK FACTORS
  Delta has yet to establish itself in the US market
  High dependence on key people

K   Conclusion

With the trend to outsourcing by the pharmaceutical companies, an investment in Delta would represent an exciting opportunity in a growth sector in a company with an excellent track record and a coherent vision. Delta could be an early float candidate on NASDAQ at a valuation appropriate to the pharmaceutical sector.

Appendix I
Due Diligence Summary

Clients work with range of agencies. Delta does not offer unique services but is regarded as a professional, high quality outfit which delivers on time.

Delta offers valuable strategic input. It is seen as a partner by its clients and not just a hired help. It also has good contacts among industry opinion leaders (i.e. leading physicians) which is an asset to clients.

Successful chemistry between the teams of the drug company and agency is vital to winning and retaining an account. It is not so much a 'predilection to a firm' as 'a predilection to individuals within that firm', according to one client.

The CEO is personally respected in the industry.

Delta is relatively expensive but quality not cost is not the main consideration in the choice of agency.

Delta is in tune with the latest technology.

No particular agency dominates the market at present. It is more a matter of one supplier dominating a particular drug company.

The US domestic market is very competitive, but Delta has the advantage of existing contacts in US pharmaceutical industry on the international marketing side. In general, outsourcing opportunities should continue to grow, especially from those drug companies with rich pipelines.

(*The rest of the Appendices listed in the Contents earlier are not included because of space limitations.*)

Glossary of Terms

AUDIT COMMITTEE: A committee of the Board vested with responsibility for reviewing a company's Accounts and Finances.

AUTHORISED INVESTMENT TRUST: An investment trust authorised by the fiscal authorities which enables investments to be traded in a tax-effective manner.

AUTHORISED UNIT TRUST: A trust authorised by the fiscal authorities which enables funds to be called up or paid out in a tax-effective manner.

BOOTSTRAPPING: Setting up a company on minimal resources and capital, in its formative phase.

CONGLOMERATE: An industrial group of companies with diverse and unrelated interests.

CONVERTIBLE DEBENTURE: A loan for a finite term made to a company, on fixed or varied interest rates, which can be converted into shares on pre-agreed terms.

CONVERTIBLE PREFERRED SHARE: Preferred share capital which can be converted into ordinary shares on pre-agreed terms.

DISCOUNTED CASH FLOW: The cash flow of a company or investment discounted back to give a net present value at today's date.

DUE DILIGENCE: The detailed research and investigation carried by a venture capital firm into a target company before making an investment.

EQUITY: A company's ordinary share capital.

219

FUND OF FUNDS: A fund which invests in a range of managed funds to give a spread of investments.

GEARING OR LEVERAGING: The ratio of debt to equity capital.

HMO: Health Management Organisation

INDEMNITIES: The giving of assurances to a purchaser against damage or loss on specified items.

INITIAL PUBLIC OFFERING (IPO): A first offer of shares by a company seeking a listing on a public market.

INTERNATIONAL NICHE BUSINESS: A company with a wide market spread and a narrow product focus.

IPR: Intellectual property rights, which should ideally be patented.

IRR: Internal rate of return per annum on an investment, calculated by working out its discounted cash flows.

IT: Information Technology.

LIMITED PARTNERSHIPS: A partnership made of limited partners with liability limited to their contributions, which is usually managed by a General Partner with unlimited liability.

M&A: Mergers and Acquisitions

NOMINATIONS COMMITTEE: A committee of the Board tasked with the reviewing and recruitment of Board members and key staff.

ONE ROUND FINANCINGS: A one-off injection of new money into a company, geared to meet its future financing needs.

PHASES I–III OF CLINICAL TRIALS: The phases of human testing which a new drug must go through before it receives regulatory approval for commercial use.

PHASE IV OF CLINICAL TRIALS: The monitoring of a new drug after its commercial launch.

REDEEMABLE DEBENTURES: Debentures or loans which are redeemable by the company and/or the lender after a definitive period.

REMUNERATION COMMITTEE: A committee of the Board responsible for reviewing and making recommendations on remuneration for directors and key staff.

REVENUES: The term used in the US for a company's turnover which is income, generated by its profit and loss items.

SECONDARY OFFERING: A subsequent offer of shares by an already quoted company.

SINGLE EUROPEAN MARKET: The plan to have a homogenous European market, with no economic or tariff barriers between member states of the European Union.

STAGFLATION: Stagnant growth coupled with high inflation.

STOCK: Another name for shares.

SWOT ANALYSIS: The analysis of a company's strengths and weaknesses related to its market opportunities and threats.

Index

222